A KNOT OF SECRETS

SURESH RAJU MALLAPU

Contents

A Day That Changed Everything

"In life, love may come in unexpected ways.
For some, it stays as a companion forever,
For some, it leaves behind cherished moments that time can't erase,
For others, it brings wounds that never heal,
And for a few, no matter how much they yearn, it remains distant.
What is love, truly?
Is it a feeling, or is it just destiny's play?
People often wonder why we seek connections beyond words,
But in those silent bonds, we discover lessons—
How to love, how to endure, how to grow.
We learn without speaking, without expecting,
And in that quiet journey, we find the essence of love."

"Good evening, listeners. Tonight, I bring you the story of a young woman I met two years ago. Her life is like a river—calm on the surface but hiding deep currents beneath. Let me take you to her world, where love and life collide in ways we never expect."

As I became addicted to listening to FM, these are the words I heard when I turned on the FM radio and realized that it was my story.

Kabir's voice fades into the background, and I can hear my heartbeat as if his words have transported me back to the beginning. This is my story.

The day started like any other. My alarm rang at 6:30 AM, dragging me out of a peaceful sleep. I groaned and hit the snooze button, letting myself doze off for five more minutes. As much as I loved my job, mornings were always tough for me. I finally managed to get up by 7:00 AM, slipping into my usual work clothes—a simple kurta and leggings from Biba company which I am so particular about.—and sipping tea by the window of my small apartment in Hyderabad. The view wasn't anything special—just a row of identical buildings and the sounds of the busy city below—but there was a certain comfort in it, in knowing that I was part of this world, moving through the same daily routines as everyone else.

My office was only a 15-minute drive away, and I liked getting there early. It wasn't that I was obsessed with work, but there was a sense of peace in the quiet hours before the office became full of chatter. I worked as a medical coder at a pharmaceutical company, a job that required precision and focus. The calmness of the early morning before anyone else arrived was something I valued. It gave me the time to settle into the rhythm of the day, to gather my thoughts before the rush.

By 8:45 AM, I was at my desk, my laptop humming to life. The office was still quiet, and the distant sound of the coffee machine was the only noise in the background. I liked this time—before the hustle and bustle began, when it was just me, my work, and the peaceful atmosphere. My desk was neat, with a small potted plant sitting in one corner and a photo of my parents in the other. I found comfort in these small details—they reminded me of home.

I got to work, diving into the task of coding patient data

with the precision I prided myself on. The work was repetitive, but there was something oddly satisfying about it. It was a predictable, methodical job, and I found solace in the routine. Each line of code, each batch of data, made the process smoother for someone out there. In some way, it felt like I was contributing to something bigger, even if the work itself was largely invisible.

At around 11:00 AM, the office started to come alive. People began greeting each other, and the smell of freshly brewed coffee filled the air. I smiled politely at the occasional "Good morning," but I mostly kept to myself. It wasn't that I didn't like my coworkers; they were all fine, but I had always been more comfortable on the sidelines. I didn't crave the constant chatter or the small talk. I preferred the quiet, the focus.

"Ananya, you should really take a break," my colleague Priya called out, peeking over my cubicle wall.

I looked up, offering a faint smile. "I will just let me finish this batch."

Priya rolled her eyes playfully. "You've said that twice already. Come on, you're going to burn out."

"I'll be fine," I said, turning my attention back to the screen. Priya meant well, but she didn't understand. For me, work wasn't just about deadlines. It was a way to stay busy, to keep my mind from wandering to thoughts I didn't want to have. Thoughts about everything else.

The day continued, each hour ticking by with its own rhythm. But then, just after lunch, my phone buzzed on my desk. I glanced at the screen and saw that it was Dad calling. My heart skipped a beat. He didn't usually call during work hours.

"Hello, Dad?" I answered, trying to keep my voice steady.

"Ananya, come home immediately," he said, his voice sharp, more urgent than usual.

I frowned, feeling a sense of unease creeping in. "Is everything okay? You sound... tense. What happened?"

"Just come home. Your mother and I will explain everything when you get here," he said, his tone leaving no room for debate.

I hesitated, not sure what to make of it. "Alright, Dad. I'll book a bus to Vizag for tonight, and I'll be there by morning."

"No," he interrupted. "Take a flight if you can. This can't wait."

His words unsettled me further. "Okay," I said, trying to stay calm. "I'll book a flight and call you once I land."

"Good. Be safe, Ananya," he said before hanging up.

I felt a wave of anxiety wash over me. Dad wasn't the kind of person to exaggerate, so if he said it was urgent, it probably was. I quickly packed up my things, my mind racing with a hundred questions. What was going on? Why did I need to leave so suddenly? Was someone sick? Oh God, why am I thinking in this way? Hope everything is good there.

I booked a cab to the airport and reached there by 6:00 PM and enquired about the next flight to Vizag. The next flight is scheduled for 7:30 PM.

"Just in Time," I thought and bought the ticket. I boarded the flight to Vizag. The one-hour journey felt like an eternity. My thoughts were all over the place, trying to figure out what could possibly be so important. When I finally landed and made my way to my parents' house, everything felt strange. The usual sounds of the house—the barking of my pet dog, the hum of the television—were absent. Instead, there was an unsettling stillness.

I walked into the living room, and there they were—Mom and Dad. Dad was sitting with his arms crossed, looking serious, while Mom was wringing her hands, her face filled with nervous energy.

"Ananya, sit down," Dad said, his tone calm but tense.

"What's going on?" I asked, sitting down on the sofa, my heart racing.

Mom opened her mouth to speak but paused. It was Dad who answered. "We've found a match for you. A groom."

I blinked, unsure if I had heard him correctly. "What?"

"You're at the right age, Ananya. Krishna is a good man, from a respectable family. This is for your future," Dad said, his voice firm.

I stared at him, my mind reeling. "But... I never said I was ready for marriage!"

"This isn't up for debate," he said, his tone final. "Krishna's family has shown interest, and we think this is the right time for you to settle down."

"But Dad," I said, my voice trembling, "I just started my career. I don't even know this person! And. I have...."

"You'll meet him soon," Dad replied, interrupting me with his commanding voice, unbothered by my protests.

Mom gently placed her hand on my shoulder. "We know this is sudden, Kanna, but Krishna is a kind man. His family is well-known. You'll be secure with him."

I looked at her, feeling a lump in my throat. "Amma, please... I need some time."

Mom sighed, her voice softening. "We're not asking you to decide now. Just meet him tomorrow and see for yourself."

I turned between them, feeling trapped. Their minds were made up. "Fine," I said, my voice barely above a whisper. "I'll meet him. But I'm not promising anything."

I made my way back to my room, the door clicking shut behind me. I leaned against it, staring at the familiar walls, now feeling colder, as though they were closing in on me. The weight of my parents' words pressed on me. I wanted to scream, to protest. This was all happening so suddenly. But I knew it wouldn't matter. My parents had made up their minds, and once they did, there was no changing it.

"They say it's time, they say it's right,
But I'm not ready to take that flight.
A heart divided, torn in two,
What am I meant to choose? What to do?"

I walked over to my bed, sitting down with clenched fists. It wasn't just the idea of marriage that troubled me—it was everything surrounding it: the uncertainty, the feeling of being pushed into something I wasn't ready for. But, most of all, it was the nagging thought that there was someone else I cared about more than I was willing to admit.

Arjun. My brother-in-law.

Arjun wasn't just family to me. He had been part of my life for as long as I could remember, and despite the years between us, there was always something that made our connection different. Arjun had a way of making me feel seen—truly seen—in a way no one else did. He was the son of my father's sister Monica, and his presence in my life had been a steady, quiet one. But over time, I found myself noticing things about him—things I couldn't ignore. His laughter filled a room with warmth, the way he always had a kind word or thoughtful gesture, the way he made me feel like I mattered. And, though I tried to push the thought aside, the feelings grew. Feelings I hadn't fully understood, and certainly hadn't allowed myself to acknowledge.

Arjun had never said anything that would hint at anything beyond our familial bond. He was respectful, always maintaining the space we shared. But, for me, it was never that simple. The quiet moments between us—the conversations that seemed to last longer than they should, the way his eyes met mine with understanding—felt like something deeper than just familial affection. And the more I tried to ignore it, the more it seemed to grow inside me.

"In moments shared, a spark would glow,
A hidden truth we both must know.
Beneath the silence, feelings bloom,
A love that whispers in the room."

I closed my eyes, trying to silence the thoughts of him, but they kept coming back. How could I think about Arjun when everything around me was changing so quickly? How could I reconcile my feelings for him with the future my parents envisioned for me? They had arranged this proposal for marriage, and they wanted me to meet someone I had never even spoken to, let alone felt anything for.

The times we had spent together—quiet evenings with family, conversations that always seemed to flow naturally, and the way he never failed to check in on me when I seemed off flashed in my memory. Those small gestures meant the world to me. But did he see me the same way? Or was I just a sister-in-law to him, someone he cared about, but not in the way I wanted?

Could I even consider marrying someone else when my heart was tangled in feelings for Arjun? If I did, would it destroy the bond we shared as a family? The uncertainty of it all weighed on me. I couldn't stop thinking about him, his smile, the way his presence calmed me.

In the silence of my room, I realized: that this decision wasn't just about marriage. It was about acknowledging my feelings for Arjun, something I had pushed aside for too long. I couldn't ignore it anymore. The next chapter of my life was unfolding too fast, but I wasn't ready to give up on what I truly wanted—not yet.

"My heart is torn between what's true,
A future that's planned and feelings I knew.
Caught in the silence, with no way to explain,
How do I love what I cannot claim?
How do I hide this burning flame?"

The Roots of the Bond

As sleep slowly covered my eyes, memories from years ago began to flash vividly in my mind. They were from the days before my graduation final year—a time filled with pressure, uncertainty, and moments I would never forget.

I sat at the dining table, surrounded by textbooks. The weight of the final exams was pressing down on me, and everything seemed so complicated. No matter how hard I tried, the words on the pages didn't make sense. I was overwhelmed, my thoughts racing.

"Why does everything seem so complicated? How am I going to remember all of this?" I murmured in frustration, my mind a whirlpool of stress.

Mom entered the room and immediately noticed the tension on my face. She sat down beside me with a kind, gentle smile.

"Anu, you've been studying for hours. Don't you think it's time for a break? Your mind needs rest, just like your body does," she said softly, concern in her voice.

I didn't respond immediately, my mind still tangled in thoughts. The pressure I was under made it hard to think clearly.

"I can't take a break, Maa. The exams are coming up soon, and I need to finish everything," I sighed, feeling the frustration grow.

Mom placed a hand on my shoulder, her voice tender yet firm. "You've always been hardworking, Anu, and I know you'll do your best. But remember, nothing is more important than your health. Take a moment to breathe, clear your mind, and then return to your studies with fresh energy."

I nodded, but the weight of my responsibilities still hung over me. A sense of anxiety continued to grip my heart, but I wasn't sure if it was just the exams or something deeper.

Soon after, Arjun entered with two cups of tea. He had a calming presence, as though his very nature could quiet the chaos around him. He placed a cup next to me and smiled warmly.

"You've been buried in books for hours. At this rate, you might just turn into one," he teased his tone light, trying to make me laugh.

I smiled tiredly, but my frustration was still evident. "It feels like I've been studying forever, but I still don't get it. There's so much to learn, and I can't remember everything," I said, feeling hopeless.

Arjun sat beside me, his voice soft but reassuring. "You're putting too much pressure on yourself. The exams are important, yes, but your health and well-being matter too. Take a break, even if it's just for a little while. Things will become clearer after you rest."

His words comforted me. There was something about him, about his presence, that always made me feel better.

"I wish it were that simple, Arjun. But I feel like I'm running out of time," I admitted quietly.

Arjun's expression softened. "You're not alone in this. You've been through tough situations before and come out stronger each time. You'll get through this, too," he reassured me.

I felt a bit lighter after hearing his words, but the pressure of exams still lingered. Arjun noticed this and smiled playfully.

"You know what always helps me clear my mind when I'm feeling overwhelmed?" he asked, his voice teasing.

I raised an eyebrow, curious. "What's that?"

"Ice cream," he grinned. "Come on, let's take a break. I'll treat you to a scoop or two."

I hesitated for a moment, then looked at Mom, who nodded gently. "Go ahead, Anu. A little break will do you good. But don't stay out too long."

With a small smile, I agreed. Arjun and I went to the ice cream shop. The evening air was warm, and as we walked, Arjun continued to tease me about my stress levels.

"I swear, ice cream fixes everything," he laughed, making me feel lighter.

I laughed too, feeling some of the tension in my chest ease as we ordered our ice creams. For the first time that day, I felt a sense of peace.

As we sat on a bench, enjoying our ice creams, I found myself smiling more than I had in days. Arjun's lighthearted nature made everything seem less overwhelming.

"The world feels a little lighter tonight,

Like the stars are whispering, 'It's alright.'
In the simplest moments, I find my peace,
A broken heart, a soul at ease."

When we finished, Arjun stood up and offered his hand to help me from the bench. "Ready to head back?" he asked, his voice soft.

I nodded, still feeling lighter from the time we spent together. He offered to drop me home, and during the drive back, I found myself stealing glances at him. My heart fluttered slightly every time our eyes met. It was a strange feeling, something I didn't fully understand.

"His presence stirs a storm inside,
A feeling that I cannot hide.
In silence, our hearts seem to speak,
A bond I never knew I'd seek."

When we reached my house, Arjun parked the car and turned to me. "You're home safe now," he said gently.

I opened the door but turned back to him. "Thanks for tonight, Arjun. I feel much better now," I said quietly.

He smiled, his eyes warm and reassuring. "I'm glad. Take care of yourself, okay?"

As I stepped out of the car and closed the door, I couldn't shake the strange flutter in my stomach. Watching him drive away, I realized there was something more to the way I felt about him, something I hadn't quite recognized before.

Later, after finishing my exams, I reflected on how much Arjun had helped me. His support had made everything easier, and I knew I couldn't have made it through without him.

The weeks flew by, and soon, my final semester exams were over. I passed with flying colors—a reward for all the sleepless nights and relentless effort. But deep down, I knew it wasn't just my determination that had brought me here; it was the unwavering support of those around me, especially Arjun.

When interview season arrived, the nervousness returned in full force. The thought of sitting before panels of interviewers felt daunting, like stepping into the unknown. Yet, as always, Arjun was there, his steady presence easing the tension.

One memory stood out vividly. It was a chilly morning, and I had an important interview. Arjun had insisted on dropping me off. As we drove, the silence in the car felt oddly comforting, like a quiet reassurance that I wasn't alone.

"Don't overthink it," he said suddenly, his voice breaking through my swirling thoughts.

I turned to him, puzzled. "What do you mean?"

He glanced at me with a calm smile. "I know you, Anu. You've prepared for this. Just trust yourself. Be confident, and everything will fall into place."

His words, steady and filled with faith, soothed the nervous flutter in my stomach. He had a way of making even the most overwhelming moments feel manageable.

Once he pulled the car into a small parking area near the venue, he looked at me with a rare seriousness. "Before you go, promise me something."

"Promise you what?" I asked, surprised.

"Promise me that you won't be so hard on yourself," he said, his tone gentle but firm. "You're capable, Anu. It's okay to stumble sometimes. But don't ever doubt your worth."

His words hit me harder than I expected. I nodded, feeling an unspoken connection between us.

"Now, go get that job," he added with a playful grin, breaking the intensity.

"His words, like whispers, soothe the storm,
A gentle touch, a tender form.
In the chaos, his calm anchors me,
A guiding light, a steadfast sea."

Weeks later, I got the call—a job offer from one of the top companies I had interviewed with. Excitement bubbled inside me as I shared the news with my family. It felt like a dream, one that had come true with hard work and the encouragement of people like Arjun.

To celebrate, Arjun suggested we take a drive. That evening, under a soft, lavender sky, we headed out to a secluded spot by the riverbank. The sound of water gently flowing mingled with the quiet hum of the evening.

"You've worked so hard for this moment," he said as we sat on the hood of the car, gazing at the rippling water. "I hope you realize how proud everyone is of you."

"I couldn't have done it alone," I replied, my voice barely above a whisper. "You were there for me, every step of the way."

He shrugged lightly, his eyes fixed on the horizon. "That's what family does, Anu."

The word "family" felt like a tether, reminding me of the

boundaries between us. Yet, at that moment, the air between us felt different—charged, almost.

"You know," I began, trying to lighten the mood, "there were moments when I wanted to give up. When it all felt too much."

"I could tell," he said, glancing at me. "But you didn't. That's what sets you apart. You're stronger than you think."

I looked down at my hands, fiddling with the edge of my scarf. "Sometimes, I don't feel strong."

Arjun leaned forward, resting his elbows on his knees. "Strength isn't about not feeling fear or doubt. It's about facing it anyway. And you've done that, over and over."

For a moment, we sat in silence, the world around us dimming as the sun sank lower.

"You've always been there for me," I said softly, breaking the stillness. "Even when I didn't ask for it."

"I always will be," he replied, his voice steady. "No matter where life takes you."

There was a pause, a delicate moment where neither of us spoke. The sound of the river filled the air, and I felt my heart beat just a little faster.

"Arjun," I started hesitantly, "what about you? What are your dreams?"

He smiled faintly, looking out at the water, his hands loosely clasped on his lap. "Dreams, huh? I suppose they've always been simple. I wanted to be a doctor—not just because it's what everyone in my family thought I'd be good at, but because I liked the idea of helping people. I wanted to be someone who could make things better, even if just a little."

The way he spoke was calm, without the weight of pride or arrogance. It was like he truly believed that doing good didn't need to be grand—it just needed to be consistent.

"You achieved that dream," I said with a small smile. "You're already doing it."

He shrugged lightly. "I guess I am. But I don't see it as a 'dream fulfilled.' It's just... life. Work is work. I do my part and leave the rest to whatever higher power's out there."

"Dreams don't need castles or skies too far,
Sometimes they live where the small joys are.
A smile, a bond, a gentle grace,
In the fleeting now, in this quiet place."

I tilted my head, watching him closely. "You make it sound so effortless."

"It's not, really," he admitted, turning his gaze toward me. "There are days when it gets overwhelming—watching patients struggle, feeling like no matter how much I do, it's never enough. But I've learned to let go of what I can't control. Life's too short to carry burdens that don't belong to you."

His words were laced with a wisdom that surprised me. He wasn't much older than me, but the way he viewed the world felt so grounded like he had already figured out something I hadn't yet.

"How do you stay so... balanced?" I asked, genuinely curious.

He chuckled softly, the sound light and unguarded. "It's not some big secret, Anu. I just try to live in the moment. I make time for what matters—whether it's my patients, my family, or even just a quiet evening like this. I don't let myself get caught up in things I can't change."

"That's easier said than done," I said, half-laughing. "I overthink everything, all the time."

He nodded, his expression softening. "I know. That's one of the things I admire about you. You care so deeply. But sometimes, you need to give yourself a break. Life isn't meant to be a constant checklist of achievements or worries."

"Is that why you seem so stress-free all the time?" I teased, though I was half-serious.

"Not stress-free," he corrected with a smile. "Just... stress-light. I have my moments too. But I've learned that it helps to have an outlet. For me, it's running or reading. Something quiet, something that reminds me to breathe."

"What do you read?" I asked, intrigued.

"Mostly novels—fiction, stories that take me to another world. And poetry, sometimes. It's amazing how a few simple lines can say so much."

I blinked, surprised. "Poetry? You don't strike me as the type."

"Why not?" he asked, grinning. "Just because I wear a white coat and deal with science all day doesn't mean I don't appreciate good words. Poetry is like medicine for the soul. Sometimes, after a long day, it's exactly what I need."

I smiled, feeling a strange warmth spread through me. Arjun wasn't just a doctor. He was someone who lived life with an openness I hadn't seen in many people.

"So, no big, extravagant dreams?" I asked again, though my tone was lighter now.

He paused, his eyes meeting mine. "Maybe my dream is just this. Being here, in this moment. Sharing it with someone who matters."

I felt my cheeks flush, but his words weren't heavy or loaded. They were simple, genuine, and undeniably him.

"You make it sound so easy," I murmured, half to myself.

He smiled again, the kind of smile that felt like home. "Maybe it is, Anu. If we let it be."

For a moment, the world seemed to quiet around us—the river's gentle flow, the soft rustle of leaves in the breeze, and the steady beat of my own heart. Arjun wasn't just a person who eased tension; he was someone who reminded me to breathe, to pause, and to live.

As we sat there, the stars beginning to dot the night sky, I realized how rare it was to meet someone who could make the world feel a little lighter just by being in it.

The Surprises of New Beginnings

Moving to the new city had been a whirlwind. New job, new apartment, new routine—it felt like there was always something to be done. At first, I was excited, but after a couple of weeks, the excitement gave way to exhaustion. Early mornings and late nights at the office left little room for anything else. I was barely managing to catch my breath when the weekend finally rolled around.

One evening, as I scrolled through my phone, a message from Arjun popped up.

"Hey, how is the new city treating you?"

I could not help but smile when I saw his name. I had not heard from him much lately. We'd both been busy with our own lives. I quickly typed back.

"It's been good, just really busy. Trying to get used to the pace, you know?"

His reply came instantly.
    "Sounds like you're drowning in work. Need a break? Maybe I'll come visit."

I couldn't believe it. He was always full of surprises. We

hadn't seen each other in a while, and though I was swamped with work, the thought of having him here for a bit made me feel strangely excited. Before I could even reply, my phone buzzed again.

"Hey, I'm outside. Got a little surprise for you."

My heart skipped a beat. I froze for a moment, unsure of what to think. Without hesitation, I swung open the door, and there he was—standing right outside with that familiar, easygoing smile, looking as calm and confident as ever.

"You came?" I asked, raising an eyebrow in disbelief.

Arjun simply shrugged, his eyes twinkling with mischief. "To surprise you…!"

I was stunned, a little touched by his spontaneity. He had always been like this—acting on impulse, doing things without second-guessing, much like the time he convinced me to climb that tree in Grandma's backyard when we were kids, despite my obvious fear of heights.

I stood there for a moment, unsure what to say. Finally, I managed, "Well, this is a nice surprise." And stepped aside to let him in, still surprised by how easily he could show up like this, without any plans or preparation. We'd always been like that, though—just making things up as we went along.

He dropped his bag by the couch and sat down. "So, how's it been? Your new life? Is the city living up to the hype?"

"Busy," I sighed, sinking into a chair. "I feel like I'm on autopilot most days. I haven't even had time to explore much yet."

"That sounds awful," he said with mock sympathy,

stretching his arms out. "I'm here to fix that, though. We're going out. No work talk, no rushing."

I couldn't help but smile at the thought of it. It felt like a good idea—just a day without any of the usual pressures.

"In quiet moments, time stands still,
A friend arrives, a heart to fill.
No need for plans, just souls that meet,
A simple gift, life feels complete."

We spent the day wandering through the city. Arjun seemed to know where all the hidden gems were, places I hadn't seen in my short time here. We had lunch at a little café near the river, and as we sat by the window, watching the water move lazily past, I couldn't remember the last time I'd felt so… relaxed.

"You know," Arjun said, his eyes scanning the menu, "it's funny how we used to be so much more carefree. Back in the village, we didn't care about anything—no deadlines, no pressure."

I laughed. "We were a little bit wild, weren't we?"

He grinned, clearly remembering. "Wild? We were like little hooligans, stealing mangoes from Grandma's tree and blaming it on the dog."

I burst out laughing, the memory so vivid that it felt like it had just happened. "I still don't know how Grandma didn't catch us that time."

"Oh, she heard you trip on the fence. I remember her yelling from across the yard, 'You two better get over here!'"

"I was trying to get away! But you were too slow, as usual," I teased, nudging him.

He pretended to be offended, but we both knew the truth. He'd always been the slower one when it came to running away from trouble. I used to laugh so hard at how he'd trip over his own feet, even when he was trying to escape from a simple game of tag.

We talked more about those childhood days, about the times we'd get into trouble at Grandma's house, how we'd make up ridiculous stories to get out of whatever we'd done wrong. The days when our biggest worry was whether we could get away with eating too many sweets before Grandma caught us.

Arjun leaned back in his chair, a nostalgic look on his face. "I still remember that day we tried to race down the hill behind Grandma's house. I swear you had a head start, Anu."

I rolled my eyes. "I did not! You were just too slow."

"Too slow?" he laughed. "You started running halfway down the hill before I even got my feet under me. I still remember how you tried to act innocent afterward."

"It wasn't my fault!" I protested, grinning. "You got distracted by that butterfly and just stood there, watching it. I had to run, or you'd have won."

He raised an eyebrow, clearly enjoying the argument. "I was trying to catch it. You should've seen the colors on that thing."

"Yeah, and you should've seen my face when I crossed the finish line first," I teased.

"I'll never let that go, you know," Arjun said with mock seriousness. "You cheated. Big time."

I laughed, the memory bringing a sense of warmth. It felt nice to be talking about those carefree days again, to be reminded that even though we'd both grown up, some things about us hadn't changed.

The day continued, and we made our way to a park nearby, finding a quiet spot on a bench. We sat there in comfortable silence for a while, watching the world go by. I could feel the tension in my shoulders starting to ease. Maybe I needed this more than I realized—a chance to step away from the constant rush and just breathe.

"I didn't think I'd like this place as much as I do," I said eventually, breaking the silence.

"Yeah, it's nice," Arjun agreed. "It's one of those places you don't notice until you stop and look around."

I nodded. Sometimes, I tended to get caught up in everything—work, the new city, the endless to-do lists. It was easy to forget that there were moments like this, moments of peace if only I took the time to notice.

As the sun began to set, we walked back to my place. Arjun dropped me off, and as I stood by the door, I realized how much I hadn't expected this visit to turn into something so special. We hadn't planned for it to be anything other than a simple catch-up, but somewhere along the way, it had turned into one of those moments I would remember for a long time.

"Thanks for coming, Arjun," I said, standing on the doorstep.

He just shrugged with a smile. "I wanted to give you something to smile about."

And just like that, he was off—heading back to his life, leaving me to reflect on how rare and simple moments like these could still mean the most.

"In every word, in every gaze,
A bond that time cannot erase.
With every step, with every sigh,
Together we stand, as days go by."

And I stepped back to my daily routine thereafter....

The Weight of Unspoken Words

Life in the city had become a blur of monotony. Each morning began with the familiar ritual: waking up before the sun, each morning felt like gearing up for a battlefield. Choosing what to wear—well, that often felt like a mini world war in itself. I'd stand before my closet, staring at the endless options and still feeling like there was nothing to wear. After a hurried breakfast, I was off to packing my lunch, and then braving the metro during peak hours. The metro rides were the worst—crowded to the point where even breathing felt like a privilege.

It felt like a giant machine, crushing us all in its relentless grind. Everyone moved with a singular focus, chasing time and money in a relentless cycle. I had become part of that tide, swept along without pause.

Amidst this routine, my phone buzzed unexpectedly one afternoon. My father's name flashed on the screen, and I quickly picked up.

"Ananya," his voice carried a cheerful tone, one I hadn't heard in a while, "you know how it's been my dream to own a house. After years of hard work—and with all your support—it's finally happened. We've bought our own house!" I felt my breath catch as his words sank in. His joy was palpable, radiating through the phone.

"And," he continued, his voice filled up with excitement, "we're arranging a housewarming function. Apply for leave and come home; there's so much to do."

His words were run over with pride, and I could feel his emotions through the call. For my father, this wasn't just about a house—it was a symbol of his hard work and resilience, built from every challenge faced and every step forward taken.

"That's wonderful news, Dad!" I exclaimed, unable to contain my happiness. "I'll put in my leave request today and start making plans."

Hanging up, I couldn't help but smile. Going home after so long, especially for something as momentous as this, filled me with anticipation. I knew how much this meant to him, and I felt a swell of pride knowing that his dream had come true.

The days leading up to my leave passed in a flurry of preparation. When the day finally arrived, I packed my bags with care, ensuring I hadn't forgotten anything for the trip home. As the train wound its way through the countryside, I found myself staring out the window, my mind drifting back to my father's voice and the pride it carried.

Reaching home, I was greeted by the warmth of familiarity—the scent of freshly prepared dishes, and the sound of bustling activity as everyone pitched in to ready the house for the ceremony. My father was at the center of it all, his energy infectious as he directed tasks and ensured every detail was perfect.

"Ananya, come here," he called out, gesturing toward a row of decorations. "What do you think of these flowers for the entrance?"

"They're beautiful, Dad," I said, smiling at his enthusiasm. "You've thought of everything, haven't you?"

He chuckled, a rare sound these days. "It's not every day you get to fulfill a lifelong dream. This has to be perfect."

As the day of the function drew nearer, the house buzzed with activity. Relatives arrived one by one, filling the space with laughter and chatter. The air was thick with the aroma of traditional dishes being prepared in the kitchen, and the sound of clanging utensils echoed through the halls.

The morning of the ceremony, I dressed in a pink lehenga specially chosen for the occasion. The fabric shimmered under the sunlight, its intricate gold embroidery weaving delicate floral patterns along the hem and blouse. Tiny beads adorned the neckline, catching the light as I moved. Wrapping a matching dupatta around my shoulders, I felt an unfamiliar mix of excitement and nervousness.

As guests began arriving, I found myself busy greeting them, exchanging pleasantries with family friends, and relatives I hadn't seen in years. My eyes kept drifting to the door, scanning the crowd for a familiar face.

This day was doubly special—not only was it the housewarming ceremony but also Ugadi, the Telugu New Year. The air was charged with a sense of renewal and joy, a celebration of fresh beginnings.

I couldn't help but think about Arjun—would he be here? He was part of my father's extended family, yet his presence always felt different, more significant. I searched the sea of faces, hoping to catch a glimpse of him, but he was nowhere to be found.

Standing by the entrance, my thoughts spilled into quiet poetry:

"Amid the crowd, I search in vain,
A heartbeat quickens a gentle strain.
Where is the face I long to see?
Why does absence feel like an eternity?"

Just as I began to lose hope, I saw him walking toward the house, flanked by his parents. His presence lit up the moment in ways I couldn't explain. Dressed in a crisp kurta, his confident stride and warm smile made my heart skip a beat.

"Arjun!" I called out, my voice louder than intended.

He turned, his smile widening when he saw me. "Ananya, you look stunning in your pink lehenga, like a delicate rose in full bloom," he said, his gaze lingering for a moment before he stepped forward to greet me.

The warmth of his presence filled a space in me that I hadn't realized was empty. We both exchanged pleasantries and soon everyone was swept up in the festivities.

Monika's Aunt, Mother of Arjun, arrived fashionably late followed by Arjun, as she often did, sweeping in with her signature blend of charm and authority. She was dressed impeccably, her saree shimmering with delicate zari work that caught the sunlight, and her sharp eyes scanned the arrangements like a hawk. At first, her comments were polite, even complimentary—a remark about how beautiful the floral decorations were, though she added they felt "a bit too modern" for such a traditional occasion.

I saw my father stiffen slightly but smiled and waved it off. He had poured so much effort into this function, and I could sense his determination to make it perfect. But as the moments passed, Monika's aunt's comments began to carry more of an edge.

Lunch was the highlight of the day, a grand feast prepared with care to match the dual occasion. Guests lined up to serve themselves, their plates filling with aromatic dishes: pulihora, gutti vankaya kura, sambhar, avakaya, and a wide array of sweets. The festive air carried the clinking of steel utensils and animated chatter as people found their seats and began enjoying the meal.

I was seated with my parents and close family, ensuring everything was running smoothly when I noticed Mounika's slightly raised voice. She was addressing one of the servers, her tone clipped.

"This is such an important function," she said, pausing by the dining table where the sweets and curries were placed. "Couldn't you have ensured the arrangements were proper? Sweets and curries side by side? That's not how things are traditionally done."

Her words weren't loud, but they were just audible enough for nearby guests to catch, and I could see my father's patience fraying. Still, he responded with a tight smile. "It's a minor thing, Mounika. Everyone seems to be enjoying the food. Let's not make it an issue."

But she wasn't ready to let it go. Crossing her arms, she tilted her head slightly, her tone sharp. "It's not just about the food, Mohan. These small things reflect how much respect you have for the occasion. A function like this is a reflection of the family's values."

I could feel the atmosphere shift, the warmth of the gathering dimming slightly as tension seeped in. My father's expression hardened, and he turned to her, his voice calm but laced with unmistakable anger.

"Respect, Mounika? Do you want to talk about respect?"

His words carried a weight that silenced the nearby chatter. "You only started showing respect when my fortunes turned."

The room fell into an uncomfortable hush. I glanced around, seeing the guests exchange uneasy glances, unsure of how to react.

Mounika Aunt's face turned red, and she straightened, her voice defensive. "What are you talking about? You're being ridiculous, Mohan."

But my father wasn't holding back anymore. "Oh, you know exactly what I'm talking about. When I lost everything before Ananya was born, where were you? You treated me like I didn't exist like I wasn't family. Do you remember how you refused to visit us? How did Latha have to face it all alone because you couldn't risk being associated with us? And now, when things are good again, you come back as if nothing happened."

Mounika Aunt's lips tightened, but her pride wouldn't let her stay silent. "That's not fair, Mohan! We all have struggles, and I was only being cautious. You can't expect people to ignore their responsibilities just to help you."

"That wasn't caution," my father shot back, his voice rising. "That was judgment. You didn't just stay away—you made sure we knew we weren't welcome. You looked down on me when I was at my lowest."

Her husband tried to step in, placing a hand on her arm, but she shrugged him off. "And what about you, Mohan?" she countered, her voice sharp as a blade. "Do you think I've forgotten how you ignored my advice back then? I told you not to make those risky investments, but you didn't listen. If you'd been more careful, you wouldn't have ended up in that situation in the first place!"

I sat frozen, my heart sinking as their words grew harsher, cutting deeper. Years of resentment poured out, and every unresolved issue, every minor slight, was dragged into the open.

"You've always been so quick to criticize but slow to help," my father said, his voice trembling with frustration. "And now, you dare to lecture me about respect and tradition?"

"And you've always been too proud to admit your mistakes," Mounika Aunt snapped. "You never valued my input, even when I was right!"

The argument spiraled, their voices growing louder and more bitter. My mother tried to intervene, her voice trembling as she pleaded for calm, but neither of them would relent.

Finally, Mounika Aunt grabbed her bag, her face a mixture of anger and hurt. "We don't need to stay where we're not valued," she said coldly. Turning to her family, she added, "Let's go."

I watched helplessly as they walked out, the festive air of the function completely shattered. The house, once filled with laughter and celebration, now felt stiflingly quiet despite the number of people still present. My father stood there, breathing heavily, the weight of years of anger and frustration etched on his face.

I caught Arjun's gaze from across the room, and for a moment, it felt like he understood the heaviness I was feeling. The day that was meant to mark a joyous beginning had instead exposed the fractures in our family, leaving behind an ache I couldn't ignore.

The guests began to quietly disperse, their faces etched with discomfort. Dad stood there, seething, his hands clenched into fists.

The house that had been filled with laughter and light just hours ago now felt cold and empty. As I watched my father's shoulders slump in defeat, my heart ached for the family we once were. And for the first time, I wondered if we could ever piece ourselves back together.

"The laughter fades, the warmth is lost,
Our family fractured, at such a cost.
Can hearts once hurt find their way?
Or will this silence forever stay?"

In The Silence Of The Years

After that incident, the house seemed engulfed in a heavy silence, as if the silence itself had taken over as the head of the family. I returned to the city to focus on my job, but Arjun never called. Each passing day felt like an eternity. As time slipped away...

Then, one night, my phone lit up, and his name appeared on the screen. My heart leaped as if the universe had finally heard my prayers. With trembling hands, I picked up the call.

"Arjun?" I whispered, my voice betraying the flood of emotions that threatened to spill.

A soft exhale followed before his voice, familiar and warm, filled the void. "Hi, Ananya."

At that moment, every ounce of pain, every sleepless night, felt worth it. "I can't believe it's you," I said, my words rushing out. "I've missed you so much, Arjun."

But before his response, I heard another voice in the background, sharp and commanding. "Arjun, who are you talking to?"

My heart sank. I knew that voice—it was Mounika Aunty, his mother. Her words were laced with an authority that left no room for defiance.

"It's... no one, Amma," he said, his tone faltering.

"Is it someone from Mohan's family?" she pressed, her voice growing colder with every word.

There was silence on the line, and then a rustle, as if he had moved away from her. But her voice persisted, louder and more insistent. "Arjun, I've told you before. I won't have you speaking to them. Do you hear me? Their pride has already caused enough damage. Don't test my patience."

Her words struck like a blow, each syllable reverberating in my chest. I wanted to scream, to tell her that I was still the same Ananya she had once welcomed with open arms. But the anger in her voice left no space for reconciliation.

I heard Arjun's soft sigh, the weariness in it breaking my heart. "Amma, please," he began, his voice pleading. "This isn't fair. Ananya—"

"Enough!" she cut him off, her tone final and unyielding. "If you respect me, Arjun, you'll end this. Now."

The silence that followed was deafening. I could almost picture him standing there, torn between his love for me and his loyalty to his mother.

"Ananya," he finally said, his voice barely above a whisper. "I'm sorry."

And then the line went dead.

They say life marches on, blind to the storms that rage in the depths of the heart. My days were a relentless cycle of formulating algorithms and coding drug compositions. As a bioinformatics professional, I worked on projects that promised to save lives, but somewhere deep inside, I felt lifeless myself. Arjun's silence had carved a hollow ache inside me—a wound that refused to heal.

In the sterile lab where I spent most of my hours, surrounded by screens and datasets, his absence loomed like a shadow. The formulas I worked on, and the intricate codes designed to model the behavior of drugs in the human body, were complex puzzles I could solve. But the puzzle of Arjun's silence? That was something I couldn't untangle, no matter how hard I tried. I drowned in the echoes of my solitude. The silence between Arjun and me had stretched unbearably thin, like a thread threatening to snap. But somewhere, deep in my heart, I still hoped—hoped that he would call, that his silence was temporary.

One night, when the weight of it all became unbearable, I left him another message.

"Arjun, I know this isn't easy for you. It isn't easy for me either. But I need you to know that I'm still here. I still care about you, no matter what. I hope... I hope someday we can find a way through this."

The message went unanswered, like so many before it. I tried to remind myself that his silence wasn't a reflection of his feelings, but of the impossible position he was in. Yet, doubt began to creep in, whispering that maybe, just maybe, I had already lost him.

"A love that lingered now feels so distant,
Was it fleeting, or truly consistent?
With each passing day, I wonder in pain,
Will we meet like before, or am I insane?"

To cope, I turned to the one thing that offered me peace: FM radio. Late at night, when the hum of lab equipment faded and the world outside my apartment felt silent, I would switch on my favorite station. The voice of RJ Kabir filled the emptiness, soothing and wise, like a friend who understood without asking.

Kabir had a way of weaving poetry into his shows, his words painting pictures of longing, resilience, and hope. I didn't know his face, but his voice became a lifeline. I found myself clinging to his monologues, replaying them in my mind long after the show had ended.

"In the stillness of the night,
When shadows whisper and dreams take flight,
A voice emerges, steady and clear,
A balm for the soul, a friend ever near."

His words felt like they were meant for me, as though he understood the pain of loving someone you couldn't reach.

Everywhere I went, I saw traces of Arjun. The café where we used to meet, the bookshop where we'd spent lazy afternoons browsing shelves, and even the research papers I read on drug simulations. His dream of becoming a surgeon intertwined with my world in unexpected ways.

One evening, I saw him. It was a fleeting moment, across a crowded street. He was wearing his white coat, his stride purposeful, his expression focused. My heart twisted at the sight. He looked every bit the man he had always wanted to be—confident, accomplished, untouchable.

I wanted to call out to him, to congratulate him, to tell him how proud I was. But I couldn't. What could I possibly say that wouldn't sound hollow? That I missed him? That I still thought about him every day? After remembering her mother's words I couldn't dare to do so and not wanted to disturb their bond.

Would Arjun ever break his silence? I didn't know. But I clung to the hope that one day, the weight of our love would bring us back to each other. Until then, I would carry him with me—in the quiet corners of my soul, in the words of Kabir, and in the unshakable belief that some connections can never truly be broken.

"The phone feels heavy in my hand,
A bridge to him, yet here I stand.
Do I risk the silence, the pain anew?
Or let him go, as I'm told to do?"

They say time heals all wounds, but for me, time was the blade that deepened the cuts. The day our families stopped talking felt like an unspoken farewell—a fracture I never anticipated. At first, I told myself it was temporary. "Two weeks, maybe three," I thought. "Arjun will call. He always does."

But days turned into weeks, weeks into months, and soon, two and a half years had slipped through my fingers like sand. I often sat by my window, staring at the road outside, hoping to see his familiar silhouette.

Every evening, as the sun dipped below the horizon, I would whisper to myself:

"Oh sun, take my heart to him today,
Let your rays find where he may lay.
Carry my silence, my unshed tears,
To the one I've missed for two long years."

I never spoke these words aloud, for they felt too vulnerable, too raw. Instead, I buried them deep, pretending I had moved on, even as my heart screamed otherwise.

And then, one day, everything changed. The call came. It wasn't from Arjun. It was from my family, urging me to come home. They had found a wedding match for me. The message was clear: *it was time to choose.* Time to step into the future and leave behind the past.

As I sit here, in the quiet of my room, thinking back on everything that has brought me to this point, I can't help but wonder—what now? What do I do with the love that still lingers, despite everything? My heart still beats for Arjun, but life moves forward. The man I'm to meet in my hometown... will he be the one to fill the void Arjun left? Will I ever be able to forget him?

The question haunts me now, as I prepare to return to the place where it all began, where my love for Arjun took root, and where the possibility of a new future lies waiting.

I don't know what I'll choose. But I know this: the story I've told you tonight—of love, loss, and silence—is far from over. The next chapter is still unwritten.

As I close my eyes tonight, I wonder—will I find Arjun again, or will the road ahead lead me somewhere else?

"The past and future call my name,
In love and loss, I'm not the same.
A choice awaits, yet I still yearn,
For a love that may never return."

Caught in the Crossroads of the Heart

The next morning, I woke up with a heaviness in my chest, as if the weight of the world was pressing down on me. I hadn't slept much the previous night. The endless thoughts, the constant replay of memories, and the looming reality of the proposal meeting today had kept me wide awake. I couldn't shake the feeling that something wasn't right. Four years had passed—four years filled with love, loss, laughter, and silence—and now, I was here, standing at the edge of a new chapter. But the question was, which chapter was this? The one where I let go of the past, or the one where the past still held me captive or my past may become a real one? Though it seemed to be impossible between the egos, respect, and anger.

I rubbed my eyes, trying to push away the exhaustion that clung to me like a second skin. But it was pointless. The proposal meeting was today, and I had to face it. My mom had been buzzing around the house for hours, making sure everything was perfect for the boy's family. Her excitement was evident, but it felt like a distant echo to me, as though I were watching everything unfold from the outside, disconnected from it all. How could I be excited? How could I even begin to think about the future when my heart still lingered in the past?

I dragged myself out of bed, feeling the weight of each step. I walked to the kitchen, my movements sluggish, as though my body didn't quite belong to me today. Mom was there, humming softly as she prepared breakfast. She looked up at me, a smile lighting up her face, but I could see the worry in her eyes too, just beneath the surface.

"You're awake early today, Anu. Good," she said, her voice cheerful. "I was just getting some things ready for the meeting later. I want everything to go perfectly."

I offered a half-hearted smile, but my heart wasn't in it. "Yes, Mom," I replied, my voice barely above a whisper. I couldn't bring myself to share her excitement. Instead, my mind was consumed with the events of the past few days—the strange flutter in my chest when I thought about Raj, the proposal that felt like a foreign concept, and the undeniable pull toward someone who wasn't here.

Mom's voice interrupted my thoughts. "Is everything ready?"

I nodded absently, though I could hardly focus on anything. "Yes, Mom." The words felt empty, disconnected from the storm inside me.

She continued to move around the kitchen, busying herself with the preparations, but I couldn't concentrate on what she was doing. I just wanted to disappear. I wanted to run away from the weight of it all. This wasn't just a proposal. This wasn't just about meeting someone new. This was about my future, a future that my family had already mapped out for me. And yet, as much as I tried to accept it, I couldn't escape the unsettling feeling that I wasn't ready. My heart still belonged to someone else. Someone who had once been everything to me.

I sat there, lost in my thoughts, my heart heavy with so

many conflicting emotions. I wasn't ready for any of this, but Mom seemed determined to make me look like I was. She walked over to me with a soft, reassuring smile, like she didn't see the storm raging inside me.

"Come on, beta," she said, her voice gentle yet firm. "It's time to get ready. You need to look your best today."

I felt a wave of resistance rise within me. *I don't feel like it, Mom,* I wanted to say, but the words didn't come. Instead, I just nodded silently as she led me toward the wardrobe. I could feel her energy, her enthusiasm, and I couldn't bring myself to break it. Even though my heart wasn't in it, I knew this was what she wanted.

When she pulled out the saree, I almost didn't believe my eyes. It was beautiful—a rich, deep red, the kind of color that demands attention and speaks of elegance, tradition, and strength. I couldn't see myself in it, but the soft silk shimmered under the light, almost as if it was inviting me to step into it, to be the woman my family expected me to be.

Mom draped the saree over my shoulders with such care, smoothing it out like it was the most precious thing she owned. She didn't say much, just moved with an ease that spoke of years of practice. Her fingers were gentle as she tied the saree, adjusting the pleats and ensuring everything fell perfectly. I couldn't help but notice how she seemed to do it without thinking, while I struggled to make sense of everything swirling inside me.

She added the pallu next, arranging it over my shoulder so it hung just right. I didn't feel like I was the one in control. It was like I was just going through the motions, letting her turn me into the version of myself I wasn't ready to be.

Then came the jewelry. She picked out a delicate gold

set, the kind that was simple but elegant. She placed the necklace around my neck, the gold warm against my skin. The earrings were small, subtle—beautiful, but not too much. It felt like she was trying to build me up piece by piece, making me something I wasn't sure I could be.

When she finished, she stood back and smiled. I turned to look at myself in the mirror, and for a moment, I didn't recognize the woman staring back at me. The saree, the jewelry, the careful way my mother had put it all together—it all seemed so... final. Like I was stepping into a life that wasn't entirely mine.

"You look beautiful," Mom said, her voice soft, but filled with such pride. She brushed a strand of hair from my face, as though to make sure every detail was perfect.

I looked at myself in the mirror, my heart still heavy. I looked different, yes. The reflection was that of a woman about to meet her future, but inside, I felt like a girl who wasn't ready to face what was coming. The saree, the jewelry—they didn't change the uncertainty in my chest. But they did make me feel like I had no choice but to face the world, even if I didn't feel ready to step into the role I was being handed.

I forced a small smile, but it didn't quite reach my eyes. I didn't know how to tell her that, no matter how stunning I looked, I wasn't sure I was ready for this. I wasn't sure I ever would be.

As the hours passed, my anxiety grew. The clock was ticking, and before I knew it, the time for the boy's family to arrive had arrived. The doorbell rang, and my heart skipped a beat. It was them. They were here. I stood frozen for a moment, unable to move. The moment felt like it was suffocating me. Was I really ready for this? Could I go through with it? My thoughts swirled in a tornado of confusion, doubt, and fear.

Mom hurried to the door, her face lighting up with excitement. I followed behind her, trying to steady my breath, my mind still racing. They were here. The boy's family was here. And I was expected to greet them like it was just another ordinary event. But how could it be? How could I pretend that everything around me was normal when my heart was in pieces?

The door opened, and standing there was a well-dressed couple—the boy's parents—followed by a tall, confident-looking man. Raj. He had an aura about him, a quiet strength that made him stand out. His posture was straight, and his eyes were warm, but there was something else there too—something I couldn't quite place. He looked at me, his smile gentle, and for a moment, my heart fluttered in a way I hadn't expected. Was this really happening? Was this the person my family had chosen for me?

He stepped forward and extended his hand. "Hello, Ananya. It's nice to meet you."

I felt a strange flutter in my chest, something that didn't feel right. It wasn't excitement or nervousness. It was a feeling of displacement like I was living someone else's life. "Hello," I managed to say, my voice trembling slightly. Why did it feel like everything around me was moving too fast as if I couldn't keep up

The meeting continued, and my mind was barely present. Mom and the boy's family engaged in polite conversation, discussing wedding plans, backgrounds, and how the two families could come together. But I stayed mostly quiet, my mind elsewhere. Every time my eyes met Raj's, I couldn't help but compare him to someone else. Someone who had once been my world. Someone who still had a hold on my heart.

"I stand before him, my heart far apart,
A quiet distance echoes in my heart.
Words fail me, I can't speak what's true,
Unready to accept, this life that's new."

"Ananya, tell us a little about yourself," Raj's father asked, breaking the silence.

I blinked, suddenly brought back to the present. My mouth went dry, and I found myself struggling to find the right words. "Well, I… I work in marketing. I enjoy reading and spending time with my family. I—" I stopped myself. It felt like I was introducing someone else. This wasn't me. This wasn't the life I had envisioned.

Raj smiled politely, but I could sense a flicker of something—maybe curiosity, maybe concern—in his eyes. I quickly averted my gaze.

"Ananya is a wonderful daughter," Mom interjected, her tone proud. "She's always been focused, hardworking, and dedicated."

I forced a smile, but the words felt hollow. Did Raj see the real me? Or was he just another face in a crowd, a person I was expected to welcome with open arms?

The conversation continued as I sat back, barely listening. My mind was a battlefield, filled with thoughts of Arjun, the boy who had once been my world. Was this my future? Was this man, this stranger, the one I was supposed to marry? My heart screamed for Arjun, but I had to push those feelings down, didn't I? This was what my family wanted. This was what was expected of me.

Later in the evening, as the boy's family left, Mom turned to me, her eyes full of anticipation. "Well, Anu? What do you think of him?"

I hesitated. How could I tell her the truth? How could I tell her that my heart was still with someone else, that I wasn't ready to let go of a past that felt so alive within me?

"He seems nice," I finally said, my voice distant, as though I were speaking from a place far away.

Mom's face softened. "Is something bothering you, beta? You're not saying much. You've been so quiet."

I looked at her, feeling the weight of the unspoken words pressing down on me. "I just... I don't know. It feels so sudden. I've never even thought about marriage like this before. I'm not sure I'm ready."

Mom sighed and sat next to me, her hand resting gently on my shoulder. "I understand, Anu. But sometimes, things happen when we least expect them. You don't have to decide anything right away. Take your time. Think it over."

I nodded, though the doubt still gnawed at me. How could I even begin to think about a future with Raj when my heart still belonged to someone else? It wasn't fair to anyone—not to Raj, not to my family, and certainly not to myself.

That night, after everyone had gone to bed, I found myself alone on the terrace. The cool night air washed over me, and the stars above seemed to reflect my turmoil. I sat with my journal, its blank pages staring back at me, urging me to release everything I had locked inside.

What was I supposed to do now? My heart was still tangled in the past, still aching for someone who wasn't here. I wasn't ready for this future. I wasn't ready to let go. My fingers hovered over the pages, and finally, the words came:

"I never thought I'd feel this way,
Caught between what I want to say.
The life I've dreamed of, the life I fear,
Is it worth it, or should I disappear?"

The words seemed to capture everything I had been feeling. The weight of my family's expectations. The longing for the past. The fear of the future. But above all, the yearning to follow my heart, even if it meant going against everything I had been taught.

The future seemed so unclear, so full of uncertainty. But one thing was certain: I couldn't let go of the past just yet.

A Voice in the Dark

The night was quiet, yet the noise inside me was deafening. The house was steeped in silence, every corner weighed down by my mother's unspoken hopes and my father's measured glances. My life felt like a carefully orchestrated play, where everyone had their roles, but my part seemed undefined—adrift.

Unable to bear the stillness, I grabbed my phone, plugged in my earphones, and tuned into the FM station that had become my only solace over the past few months. A deep, warm voice filled the emptiness, wrapping around me like a comforting embrace. It was Kabir, the RJ whose words seemed to echo my hidden thoughts.

His voice was poetry, his tone a melody that carried me away from my turmoil. Tonight, his words seemed almost prophetic:

"Have you ever felt like you're standing at the edge of a cliff, unsure whether to leap into the unknown or step back into the familiar? The heart yearns for answers, but sometimes, silence becomes its loudest companion."

I froze. How did he know? How could he articulate what I couldn't? My breath hitched as he continued.

"Loneliness isn't just being alone; it's the ache of feeling unseen,

unheard. But remember, even the darkest night whispers secrets to those who dare to listen."

Tears welled up in my eyes. I wasn't sure if they were from relief, validation, or sheer exhaustion. For the first time in months, someone had voiced what I couldn't, even if that someone was a stranger speaking into a microphone miles away.

The next day, I couldn't shake the thought of Kabir. His words had sparked something in me—a desire to be heard, to share the storm inside. Driven by an inexplicable urge, I found myself searching for the FM station's official website. It didn't take long to find a contact number listed.

It was bold, maybe even reckless, but I called the number. My hands trembled as I waited for someone to pick me up.

"Hello, this is RJ Kabir's desk. How may I help you?" a polite voice answered.

"I… I need to speak to him," I stammered, unsure if this was even allowed.

The assistant hesitated but eventually replied, "I'll pass your message along. He usually responds to such requests personally. Can I take your name?"

I hesitated before whispering, "Ananya."

True to their word, Kabir called back the next day. Hearing his voice again, this time directed at me sent a shiver down my spine.

"This is Kabir," he said. His tone was calm and reassuring. "You wanted to talk?"

"Yes," I began, my voice shaky. "I'm sorry for bothering

you, but… your show, your words—they felt like they were speaking directly to me. I didn't know who else to turn to."

There was a pause, and then his voice softened. "No apologies, Ananya. Sometimes, we need to unburden ourselves to someone who isn't entangled in our lives. What's on your mind?"

The dam broke. I poured my heart out, recounting everything—Arjun, the silence between us, the family rift, the lingering ache of unresolved emotions, and the suffocating expectations of my parents.

"I feel like I'm stuck," I admitted, my voice cracking. "I don't know how to move forward when my past still pulls me back. And I'm scared… scared that I'll never find my way."

Kabir listened without interruption, his silence a comforting presence. When I finally finished, he spoke with the wisdom of someone who had seen life's complexities unfold.

"Ananya," he said, his voice gentle but firm, *"healing isn't about forgetting; it's about learning to carry the pain differently. The heart may ache for what it once had, but sometimes, it's in the ache that we discover our strength."*

I closed my eyes, letting his words sink in.

"You're searching for answers outside yourself," he continued. *"But what if the answers have been within you all along? What if the clarity you seek comes not from closure with someone else, but from making peace with yourself?"*

His words struck a chord deep within me. Could it really be that simple? Could my salvation lie in my own hands?

Over the next few weeks, Kabir became an unexpected anchor in my turbulent life. I found myself calling his station regularly—not for advice, but to listen, to learn, and to rediscover parts of myself I had forgotten.

His shows, laced with poetry and reflection, became my nightly ritual. Each word felt like a tiny beacon, guiding me through the dark.

"The stars above don't fight the night,
They simply shine with all their might.
So too must you, dear heart of mine,
Embrace the dark, and let yourself shine."

His voice was my balm, his words my guide. And though I didn't know where this journey would lead, for the first time in a long time, I felt like I was finally taking the first steps toward finding myself again.

It took time, but I finally gathered the courage to speak with my parents. I waited for the right moment, knowing this conversation would not be easy. One evening, as my father was sipping tea and my mother was going over the day's chores, I sat them down.

"I need to talk to you both," I began, my voice steady despite the storm brewing within me.

My father's brow furrowed. "What is it, Ananya?" he asked, his tone cautious.

"It's about the proposal," I said. "I... I don't think I'm ready for this."

My mother's hands froze mid-motion, and she exchanged a worried glance with my father. "What do you mean you're not ready?" she asked, her voice tinged with concern.

"I feel conflicted," I admitted. "I need more time to think about what I truly want. This decision feels too rushed."

My father's face darkened, his voice taking on a stern edge. "Ananya, marriage is not something you overthink. It's about practicality, compatibility, and family values. Raj's family is perfect for us—for you."

"But, Dad," I interrupted, "what if it doesn't feel right to me? Shouldn't my feelings matter too?"

"Your feelings?" he scoffed, his tone dripping with disbelief. "Do you think your mother and I had the luxury of over-analyzing our marriage? We trusted our families, and look where we are today."

"Times have changed, Dad," I argued, my voice trembling. "I'm not saying I'll never get married. I'm just asking for more time to figure things out."

My mother's voice broke through, softer but no less insistent. "Ananya, you've always been a good daughter. Don't you trust us to make the right decision for you?"

Before I could respond, my father's phone rang. He glanced at the screen, his expression softening as he answered. It was Raj's parents. As he spoke to them, a smile crept across his face, one I hadn't seen in a while. After exchanging pleasantries, he hung up and turned to us with a definitive tone.

"They've given their approval," he announced. "Raj and his parents are happy with the proposal and want to proceed further. I think it's time we finalize the engagement date."

"Dad, please wait," I interjected, feeling the weight of urgency press against my chest. "I need to tell you something important first."

My mother looked at me, a mixture of curiosity and concern in her eyes, while my father frowned slightly but gestured for me to continue.

"I've been carrying a lot inside me," I began, my voice quivering but resolute. "It's about Arjun."

My mother's face paled, and my father's brows furrowed deeply. "What about Arjun?" he asked cautiously.

"I've had feelings for him," I admitted, the words feeling heavy yet liberating as they left my mouth. "For a long time. And even though nothing came of it, those feelings haven't just vanished. I need you to understand that I cannot marry Raj because I'm in love with Arjun."

The room fell into an uncomfortable silence, the kind that weighs down every word yet to be spoken. My mother finally broke it, her voice trembling with disbelief. "Ananya, why didn't you tell us earlier? We could've—"

"What could we have done?" my father interrupted, his tone sharp. "This isn't just about your feelings; it's about maintaining harmony. The dispute from the housewarming hasn't been resolved in my mind yet. And now, you're jeopardizing a perfectly good match because of something that won't be happening."

"It's not just something," I countered, my voice firm despite the tears brimming in my eyes. "It's my life, Dad. My emotions. Don't they matter? Don't I matter in this decision?"

My father's expression hardened. "Ananya, this is absurd! Have you forgotten the history between our families? The disputes, the disagreements? Arjun is out of the question, and I won't hear another word about it."

"But, Dad—"

"No!" he snapped, rising from his chair. "This discussion is over. You will marry Raj. That's final."

My mother tried to intervene, her voice soft but urgent. "Mohan, let's think this through—"

"There's nothing to think through, Latha," he said, his tone cutting. "Ananya is letting her emotions cloud her judgment. I won't allow this family to be dragged into another mess."

Tears streamed down my face as I looked at my father, his anger as unyielding as a stone wall. "Dad, please," I whispered, my voice breaking. "I need you to understand—"

But he had already turned away, signaling the end of the conversation. My mother stood frozen, torn between her husband's authority and her daughter's pleas. And I caught in the middle, felt the weight of my truth suffocating me.

For the first time, I realized that speaking my truth didn't mean it would be accepted. But at least, for once, I had found the courage to speak it aloud.

"The past still whispers, sharp and clear,
A future shaped by silent fear.
In breaking hearts, a truth untold,
Yet strength is found where love's been cold."

The Unheard Plea

The sharp rejection from my father still echoed in my mind. I couldn't make sense of it. Despite all my efforts, despite everything I had tried to explain, my father's anger had cut through all understanding. He had been so steadfast in his refusal to even hear me out, so cold, that it felt like the warmth of our bond had been snuffed out in an instant. The very person I had looked up to, the one who had always been my pillar of support, had turned away from me. The words "I don't understand you anymore" were a dagger to my heart, and I was left reeling, unsure of what to do next.

Confusion overwhelmed me. How could things have gotten so twisted? I was torn between my love for Arjun and the obligations my family had placed on me. I needed someone to talk to, someone who would understand, someone who wouldn't judge me. I reached for my phone, my fingers trembling as I unlocked it. The screen lit up, and I saw Kabir's contact name.

I took a deep breath and pressed the call button. "Hi Kabir," I said, my voice shaky, barely above a whisper.

"Hi, Ananya. How are you?" he replied, his voice as comforting as always. But I could hear the concern in his tone, and I knew he sensed something was wrong.

I wasted no time and began recounting everything—every

single word, every look, every rejection. I shared the conversation with my father, the silence in the room as my father's anger had grown, and how my mother, despite being silent, had sided with him in the end. I described how, with no more words left to say, my father had simply walked away, leaving me standing there, confused and lost.

Kabir listened patiently, his silence offering me the space I needed to express the overwhelming emotions I had bottled up. When I was done, I let out a shaky breath. "What should I do, Kabir? I don't know what to think anymore."

There was a long pause on the other end of the line. I could feel him taking his time, choosing his words carefully. Then, with a firm yet compassionate tone, he spoke, "It's been like this for years, Ananya. I know it feels impossible right now, but you have to fight for what you love. Don't let this silence define you. Leave the rest to fate. If your love is true, it will find a way through. Sometimes, fate has its own timing, and we can't control it. But you can control what's in your heart."

His words, though comforting, didn't bring the clarity I was hoping for. But they did provide me with a sense of strength I hadn't known I needed. "Thank you, Kabir. You always know what to say," I whispered, feeling the weight of his encouragement sink into my bones.

Later that day, something unexpected happened. As I was heading towards the hall, still in my thoughts, I noticed Raj standing there, waiting. His presence startled me a little. Before I could even react, he approached me with a tentative smile.

"Good morning, Ananya. I was hoping we could talk. I've been thinking... Would you like to go out to a café with me? Maybe we can talk more," he asked, his voice soft but filled with a kind of uncertainty.

I didn't know how to respond at first. I didn't want to hurt him, but I wasn't sure how much longer I could keep up the pretense. My mother, from the kitchen, noticed the conversation and subtly gestured for me to go. It was as if she wanted me to make the most of this time with him, even though my heart wasn't in it.

I gave Raj a tight smile. "Sure. Let's go," I said, forcing the words out as my mind was still clouded with thoughts of Arjun, my father, and my own conflicted feelings.

We drove to a nearby café, and as we sat down, Raj tried his best to engage me in conversation. He spoke about his work, his hobbies, and his favorite places to visit, but I couldn't focus on his words. My mind kept drifting, thinking about Arjun, about the fight with my father, and about what I was supposed to do with my life now that everything seemed so uncertain.

"A truth too heavy, I've yet to say,
In love with him, I've lost my way.
Yet fate spins a web I cannot escape,
As I drown in choices, too hard to make"

Finally, I couldn't hold it in anymore. I interrupted him, my voice trembling. "I need to tell you something, Raj. Something important."

He looked up, his eyes filled with hope and curiosity. "Yes, of course, Ananya. What is it?"

I took a deep breath, trying to steady myself, but the words came out in a rush. "I'm in love with someone else," I blurted out. "I don't want to hurt you, but I have to be honest. I can't move forward with this proposal. I can't marry you while I'm still thinking about him."

There was a long, painful silence. Raj sat there, staring at me, his face frozen in shock. I could see the hurt in his eyes, but it didn't matter. I couldn't lie anymore. I couldn't go on pretending that I didn't have someone else in my heart.

He didn't say anything at first. After a moment, he quietly stood up, his chair scraping against the floor. "I... I understand," he said softly. "Thank you for being honest, Ananya. I'll leave you to it. Take care of yourself."

Without another word, he turned and walked away. I watched him leave, a strange mixture of guilt and relief flooding through me. It wasn't the easy way out, but it was the only way I could be true to myself.

That evening, when I returned home, the house was filled with an odd kind of energy. My mother was bustling around, and I could hear the sound of people talking in the background. I went to ask her what was going on, and to my shock, she told me that tomorrow was my engagement day. And just like that, she dropped the bombshell: within a month, they would be fixing the marriage date as well.

I felt as though the ground had shifted beneath me. My heart dropped as I processed the news. How could this be happening? How could they move forward so quickly, with no regard for my feelings, after everything I had just shared? I had pleaded with Raj to cancel the proposal, yet here I was, standing at the edge of a future I didn't want.

My father's rejection, my mother's quiet acceptance, Raj's confusion—it all felt like a cruel game I was stuck in. And worst of all, I wasn't even allowed a choice in the matter.

"Fate weaves its threads in tangled strands,
A web of love and rejection it demands.
I plead for freedom, yet it pulls me near,
A twisted game, my heart unclear."

Threads of Fate, Knots of Love

The weight of my thoughts pressed heavily on my chest as I sat on the edge of my bed, staring at nothing in particular. *"What the hell is wrong with my life?"* I screamed silently, biting my lip to stifle the tears threatening to escape. Fate was cruel, unrelenting, playing with me like a puppet on its strings.

"Where is Arjun? Does he even care about how I am struggling?" I shouted silently, my fists clenching the sheets. "Is there anyone who can help me get my loved one back?" I murmured under my breath, the despair sinking deeper.

And then, like a ray of light cutting through storm clouds, a flicker of hope amidst the chaos- a thought struck me. Arjun's father, Hemanth uncle. He had always been close to my father once upon a time. Maybe, just maybe, he could help. It was my last chance, the only thread of hope I could cling to. Without overthinking, I decided to visit him. My heart clenched at the decision. What if he refused? What if this effort only worsened things? But the flicker of hope was enough to push me forward.

"When the path seems endless, lost in despair,
A faint light beckons, fragile yet fair.
Hope whispers softly, "Don't let it go,"
For even in darkness, seeds of courage grow"

As I approached their house, my heart raced like a frightened bird, fluttering against the cage of my chest. The house bustled with activity, voices and sounds spilling out into the courtyard. Something was definitely happening. My mind spiraled into overdrive.

Is his engagement taking place? My brain swirled with overthinking. My heart began to falter, fainting with every beat. Each step toward the door felt like climbing a mountain, my legs shaky and unsteady.

Inside, the familiar warmth of the house struck me, but it felt foreign now, overshadowed by my apprehension. I saw Mounika aunt busy in the kitchen, preparing meals with practiced efficiency. My legs nearly gave out at the sight of her. "If she spotted me, she'd surely lash out," I thought, whispering to myself, fear creeping into my resolve. My eyes scanned the room, desperately searching for Arjun, but he was nowhere to be seen. The air was thick with tension, or maybe it was just my own unease painting everything in shades of dread.

The sound of footsteps descending the stairs drew my attention. It was Hemanth uncle. I gathered all my courage and approached him, greeting him with a hesitant smile. He looked shocked to see me but recovered quickly, his kind demeanor returning.

"Hi, Anu! How are you? How is everyone in the family?" he asked warmly, though his voice carried a hint of curiosity.

"Everyone is fine, uncle. What's going on here? Are you hosting any function?" I asked, unable to mask my curiosity.

"No, Arjun is returning from Australia after completing his PhD in medical sciences," he replied, a proud smile lighting up his face.

Relief washed over me like a tidal wave. *Phew... what a relief.* My heart regained its rhythm. "Did he come yet?" I asked, barely able to contain my eagerness.

"Not yet. We're all waiting for him," he said.

Just then, Mounika aunt entered the room, her gaze landing on me. Her expression hardened, laced with sarcasm and anger. She greeted me curtly, and I braced myself for her sharp words.

Amid the tension, the door creaked open, and there he was—Arjun. His presence filled the room, and for a moment, everything else faded away. My heart skipped a beat, but I quickly turned back to Hemanth uncle.

"Uncle, I need to talk to you. Can you please listen to me?" I implored, my voice trembling with urgency.

"Yes, ma. What's the matter?" he asked, his tone calm and reassuring.

The words burst out of me before I could think. "Uncle, I am in love with Arjun. I can't forget him. I know our families had disputes four years ago, but I can't imagine my life without him. Please talk to my father. I am begging you." Tears spilled freely down my cheeks, each drop carrying the weight of my emotions.

Mounika aunt erupted. "Why are you acting? What's your plan now? Humiliating my family again?" she shouted, her voice sharp and accusing.

Hemanth uncle intervened, his voice firm yet composed. "Mounika, don't jump to conclusions. Anu has come here with sincerity. Listen to her before making judgments."

"Sincerity?" Mounika scoffed, her tone dripping with

sarcasm. "Where was this sincerity when her father insulted our family? You expect me to forget everything and act like nothing happened?"

"Enough, Mounika," Hemanth said, his voice rising slightly. "We know Anu from her childhood. She's humble and well-mannered. Both of them grew up together. Holding onto grudges will get us nowhere. Anu is not to blame for what happened between her father and you. Times have changed, and so should we."

Time is a river, a ceaseless flow, Washing away the grudges we sow. In love's embrace, let's begin anew, Bridging the chasm between me and you.

"Changed? After all the humiliation we faced, you want me to simply accept her?" Mounika snapped, her eyes narrowing. "You think this will magically fix everything?"

"Yes, I do," Hemanth replied, his gaze unwavering. "This marriage could bring peace to both families. Isn't that what we all want deep down? To move past the bitterness?"

Mounika hesitated, her expression softening slightly as doubt crept in. "And what if her father refuses? What if this creates more chaos?"

"I'll handle her father," Hemanth assured her. "But I need you to trust me on this. Trust that this decision is for the betterment of everyone, especially for Arjun."

After a tense silence, Mounika let out a reluctant sigh. "Fine. But if this backfires, don't say I didn't warn you."

Hemanth nodded, a small smile of relief tugging at his lips. "Thank you, Mounika. This means more than you know."

From the corner of my eye, I noticed Arjun standing at the

doorway, silently listening to the entire conversation. He didn't utter a word, his face a mix of emotions I couldn't decipher.

Hemanth uncle turned to him. "Arjun, Anu loves you, and I believe she's the perfect match for you. This marriage can mend what was broken."

"Papa…" Arjun began, but his father cut him off.

"I will take care of everything. Don't worry." He turned to me and said, "You could have told me this years ago, and things might have been different then."

My heart soared, joy bubbling up within me. For the first time in what felt like forever, I felt hope. Still, something about Arjun's expression nagged at me, but I brushed it off, assuming he was just tired from his journey.

That evening, Hemanth uncle visited my house, determination etched on his face. He greeted my father with a warm smile, but his tone carried the weight of urgency as he began the conversation. "Mohan, it's been too long since we sat together like this," Hemanth started, easing into the subject.

My father nodded, a wary expression clouding his features. "Yes, Hemanth. Times have changed. So, what brings you here today?"

Hemanth took a deep breath, choosing his words carefully. "Mohan, I came here with a request, not for myself, but for our children. Ananya loves Arjun. She's come to me with a sincere heart, asking for my help."

My father stiffened, his brows furrowing. "Hemanth, you know the history between our families. How can I overlook everything that happened?"

Hemanth leaned forward, his voice calm yet resolute. "Mohan, holding onto the past will only perpetuate the pain. Ananya and Arjun had nothing to do with our disputes. This marriage could be a new beginning for both our families."

"But what if it stirs up old wounds? What if this union only causes more conflict?" my father countered, his skepticism evident.

"I understand your hesitation," Hemanth replied, his gaze steady. "But I see this as an opportunity for healing. Ananya is a wonderful girl, and she truly cares for Arjun. This isn't just about them; it's about us finding peace after all these years."

My mother, Latha, who had been silently listening, chimed in. "Mohan, maybe Hemanth is right. Ananya has been so restless these past weeks. I've seen her struggle with her feelings. Perhaps this is the right step forward."

Mohan looked at Latha, his resolve softening slightly. "Do You think this is the right decision?"

"I do," Latha said gently. "Our children deserve happiness. Let's not let our past mistakes dictate their future."

Paths once divided, can intertwine, Healing wounds with love divine. A union forged from broken ties, Like a phoenix, our hopes will rise.

After a long silence, my father finally sighed, the tension easing from his shoulders. "Alright, Hemanth. If you're willing to move forward, so am I. Let's fix this marriage and let bygones be bygones."

A wave of relief washed over me as I overheard their

conversation from the hallway. The date was set, and the air seemed lighter with the promise of a brighter future. My heart swelled with gratitude for the persistence and understanding that had paved the way for this moment.

My heart floated on cloud nine. There was no stopping my happiness. Finally, I was going to marry the love of my life. How lucky I was! Yet, as I sat in my room, a thought crept in.

How does Arjun feel about all this? Is he happy? Unable to contain myself, I picked up my phone and called him. The phone rang, but he didn't answer.

"Whispers of love that the heart can't deny,
Dreams like clouds in the evening sky.
But silence lingers, a question remains,
Does his heart echo mine, or feel the chains?"

I stared at the phone, willing it to ring back. My excitement and unease danced together, a bittersweet rhythm that left me restless. I tried to push the doubts aside. *Maybe he's just tired from the flight. He'll call me tomorrow,* I reassured myself, but a small seed of worry had taken root in my heart.

The Sacred Hours of Love and Tradition

The morning sun filtered through the coconut trees, casting a warm golden glow over the courtyard. The air buzzed with excitement as relatives and friends bustled around, setting up for the Haldi ceremony. The courtyard was transformed into a vibrant haven of yellows and oranges, with marigold garlands draped from every possible corner. A brass pot filled with turmeric water sat at the center, its golden hue shimmering under the sunlight. This was the beginning of my journey as a bride, a moment steeped in tradition, love, and bittersweet anticipation.

I sat cross-legged on a low wooden stool, draped in a simple yet elegant yellow saree—a shade chosen to symbolize prosperity and happiness. My hair was tied back in a loose braid adorned with jasmine flowers, their fragrance calming my racing heart. Around me, the women of the house prepared the turmeric paste, grinding fresh turmeric roots with sandalwood and rose water. Their laughter was infectious, filling the space with warmth and joy. The paste, a rich golden-yellow, glistened as it was mixed to the right consistency.

As the women approached me, holding the paste in small silver bowls, my heart skipped a beat. My closest cousin, Neha, was the first to apply the turmeric. With a wide grin, she smeared the paste on my cheeks, her touch gentle yet deliberate. "For a glowing bride!" she teased, her voice ringing with affection. I laughed, but inside, I felt the gravity of the moment. Each stroke of turmeric felt like a layer of my old self being gently stripped away, revealing a new identity waiting to emerge.

"Golden hues on my skin they lay,
Whispers of dawn, a new bride's day.
Laughter spills, like a river flows,
In marigold dreams, the future glows".

One by one, the elders joined in. My aunts, each with their unique style of teasing, smeared the paste on my arms and feet. Their hands moved with a practiced grace, their fingers warm and comforting. My mother's turn came next. She knelt before me, her eyes glistening with unshed tears. Her hands trembled slightly as she applied the paste to my forehead, her touch lingering as if reluctant to let go.

"Oh, turmeric, sacred and divine,
Blessed by Lakshmi, your glow does shine.
A golden shield from evil's gaze,
A bride's first step in Lord Vishnu's praise."

The ceremony ended with a symbolic cleansing. Buckets of warm water, infused with rose petals, were brought out. My mother and aunts helped me wash off the turmeric, their hands gentle as they poured the fragrant water over me. The water felt soothing against my skin, washing away not just the turmeric but also the lingering doubts in my mind. Once the cleansing was complete, I was wrapped in a fresh saree, its bright yellow matching the glow of my skin.

The Haldi ceremony wasn't just a ritual; it was a profound experience that connected me to my roots, my family, and the countless women who had walked this path before me. As I stepped out of the courtyard, the sun now high in the sky, I felt a mix of emotions—joy, anticipation, and a quiet resolve to face whatever lay ahead. "This is it," I thought, clutching the edges of my saree. "The first step into a new life. And I am ready."

The mehendi ceremony is like a quiet prayer painted on my skin, each intricate design telling a story of love and commitment. As the henna artist's cone traces patterns on my palms, I can't help but wonder—will these designs be as permanent as the vows I'm about to take? The golden glow of the lamps in the room flickers, casting shadows that seem to dance like the spirits of the past—perhaps my ancestors, watching me, waiting for me to step into a role I've never truly known.

As the intricate mehendi designs are painted on my palms, each delicate swirl and curve seems to tell a story—one that is woven with love, destiny, and trials. The henna's rich color deepens with each passing minute, and I can't help but reflect on how this moment feels like a quiet prelude to something much bigger. There's a certain peace in the art being drawn onto my hands, but deep within, my heart wrestles with the complexity of what lies ahead.

I think about the ancient swayamvara of Sita, a story that has always been a part of our cultural fabric. Like the many kings and princes who arrived at her swayamvara, each bringing their strength and glory, I too have had my share of challenges. In Sita's story, the mighty Shiva bow stood as a test of fate. Many tried to lift it, each thinking they were worthy, each believing they were the right one. Yet, it was only Rama, with his pure heart, his devotion, and his destiny in alignment, who could lift the bow. He was the one who proved to the world that he and Sita were meant to be, that the trials were not to break them but to strengthen their bond.

And now, as I sit here at my mehendi ceremony, I feel

the weight of that same sense of destiny. Like the kings who tried but failed, Arjun and I have faced many hurdles. There were times when it felt like our love was being tested, moments when doubt crept in, and the path forward seemed unclear. The pressures of family, tradition, and my internal conflict all played their part, just as the suitors at Sita's swayamvara were tested by the mighty bow. Yet, I believe, just like Rama who was destined to lift the bow, Arjun and I are destined to overcome every obstacle in our path.

There were moments when I wondered if our love would survive the weight of expectations and if we would be able to break free from the chains of tradition and step into a future that was ours. But, much like how the bow in Sita's swayamvara was not just about strength, but about who was truly meant to wield it, I believe that our journey together has been written by the stars. The trials we've faced were not signs of defeat, but of our resilience, our ability to endure and persevere.

"Like Sita, tested by the bow's might,
Only one heart, pure and right.
Arjun, my Rama, through trials we've stood,
Together, destined, as love should."

As I sit here, watching the mehendi artist work with such precision, I am reminded of the symbolism of this ritual. The designs on my hands are intricate, much like the path that Arjun and I have walked together. Every turn, every swirl, reflects the love and the challenges that have shaped us. But, just as Sita's fate was sealed when Rama lifted the bow, I feel my fate aligning with Arjun's now. The mehendi, which darkens as it sets, feels like a mark of permanence—of commitment, of union, and of love that is as strong as the bond between Rama and Sita.

"As the henna weaves its tale of grace,
Like the lotus blooms in Lord Vishnu's embrace.

In every swirl, a goddess's dance,
Binding love with fate, a sacred trance"

Cousins giggle beside me, their laughter like the soft rhythm of temple bells, as they point out the tiny initials of the groom hidden in the designs. It's a reminder of what's to come, but it feels like an anchor, pulling me deeper into a current I can't control. My smile is forced. The jasmine in my braid, so intoxicatingly sweet, reminds me of Lakshmi—the goddess of wealth, but also of the burdens she carries. Her gaze is one of grace, but there is strength in it too. My mother, watching me with misty eyes, is the goddess in my life. She sees everything, and understands everything, but never speaks her true heart. I wonder if she's reminiscing about my childhood, about the moments when I needed her, the moments I'd never let go of.

Today, I am not just preparing to be a bride. I am preparing to step into a new chapter, one that is filled with love, honor, and destiny. Just as Rama lifted the bow for Sita, Arjun and I have overcome the tests that life has thrown at us, and now we are ready to face the world as one.

The morning of the vratham ceremony is heavy with the weight of expectation. Clad in a nine-yard saree, I sit beside my parents, and the air feels thick with incense and sacred chants. The yellow turmeric thread around my forehead feels like the protective hands of Parvati, shielding me from the unknown, yet the weight of the tradition is suffocating. As my father ties another sacred thread around my wrist, his hands tremble. His love for me is a constant, but this gesture feels like a silent goodbye. The priest's mantras float in the air, but I can barely hear them over the rush of emotions in my chest.

My mother, ever the silent strength, whispers blessings I can barely catch. She is my Lakshmi, the goddess who nurtures and protects. But as I sit there, receiving their love,

I wonder if I'm leaving them behind. Am I abandoning the home I've known, or are they sending me forward, like a river being released into the ocean—both hesitant and inevitable?

"The turmeric thread, like Ganga's flow,
Binding me to roots I've always known.
In my father's hands, the future sways,
A sacred bond, in the ancient ways."

This moment feels like a veiled blessing and a whispered farewell. Am I walking the path of Draupadi, bound by duty, or is this my journey, where I must discover my power and grace? The threads tied around me feel like the ropes that bound Arjuna's bow, a weapon of duty that I cannot let go of. But what if I no longer wish to fight this battle?

The Sangeet is meant to be a celebration—a joyous occasion where music and dance swirl around me like the rhythms of the universe. Yet, I feel like an outsider, a spectator to my own story. The lehenga I wear flows around me, but my feet feel heavy as if I'm walking the path of Draupadi, the woman whose life was never her own. She too was celebrated, her beauty admired, but did she ever feel truly free?

The music rises in the air, and for a moment, I feel the pull of something light. My friends drag me into a dance, and I laugh—laugh—for the first time in weeks. It's a fleeting moment of freedom, like Krishna's playful leelas with the gopis. I lose myself in the music, my body moving with the rhythm as if I am one with the divine dance of life. But as quickly as it comes, the joy fades. Arjun. His name lingers in my mind. Would he have joined me in this dance, or would he have stayed at the edge, silently watching? His silence speaks louder than the music that surrounds me, a constant reminder of the love that once was.

"In the dance, Krishna plays his flute,
He twirls the gopis in joyful pursuit.
But I, like Radha, stand apart,
Watching the rhythm, holding my heart."

Amid this celebration, I feel a quiet, unspoken longing—much like the longing of Radha, who loved Krishna with all her heart but was never fully embraced by him. It's as if my heart knows this dance is a prelude to something I haven't fully understood yet.

And finally, I'm living the big day that I have dreamed of—to become the wife of the love of my life. My mother and aunts are preparing me as a bride. But the absence of Arjun's presence weighs heavily in my heart. Since the day we agreed to this marriage, there has been no word from him. His silence has been like a shadow, lingering in the background of my every moment. The day we discussed our future together, I felt certain. But now, with the wedding looming, his absence feels like a gaping void, one that no amount of traditional beauty or ceremony can fill.

A Promise in the Dark

The morning light filters softly through the windows, casting a golden hue over everything in the room. My heart is a jumble of excitement and uncertainty, as I sit on the low stool, looking at myself in the mirror. Today, I will become a bride. I've heard that phrase a thousand times, but today it feels different—real, almost surreal.

I sit still as my mother moves behind me, her hands working with practiced grace. Her fingers, which have always been my comfort, are now preparing me for something that feels both ancient and new. The air around us is filled with the fragrance of jasmine flowers—fresh and sweet. They are woven into my hair, each flower placed with care. My hair, which has always been long and free, is transformed into a thick braid. My mother works her hands through my strands, intertwining the jasmine and securing it with a fine thread. I can feel the weight of the flowers as they rest against my neck, and it's as if, with each delicate bloom, I'm being tied to something greater—an unspoken promise of purity, of grace.

The jasmine blooms, my hair adorned,
Like Ganga's flow, a life is reborn.
In every braid, a story spun,
Of love, of grace, of what's to come.

Her hands are steady, but I can sense the quietness in the

room. The hum of the morning feels distant, almost sacred, as she ties the flowers. I am no longer the girl who once ran through the fields with wild abandon. I am becoming something more—a symbol of tradition, a part of something much larger than myself.

Next, she takes a small yellow thread—simple, yet profound. She holds it in her hands like an offering to the gods and ties it gently around my forehead. The thread feels snug, not tight but firm, a reminder of the responsibilities I am about to embrace. It's a turmeric-yellow, a color that shines with the blessings of Lakshmi, the goddess of wealth and prosperity. My mother's fingers tremble ever so slightly as she secures the knot, and I wonder if she's thinking of her wedding day, of her mother tying the same thread around her forehead.

The yellow thread, a sacred tie,
Under Lakshmi's watchful eye.
Bound by love, by tradition's call,
I stand as one, embracing all.

As the yellow thread settles into place, I feel a strange sense of protection. It's as if I am being shielded—not just by the thread, but by the generations of women before me. The strength of my mother, my grandmothers, and their mothers all entwined in this one simple gesture. I am no longer just a daughter; I am a vessel of tradition, a bridge between past and future.

Then, my mother reaches for the small vial of black kajal. My heart skips a beat. This is the final touch—the black dot that will mark me as a bride. I have seen this dot on so many women, from my aunts to my mother, and it always seemed like such a small thing. But today, as my mother dips her finger into the kajal and presses it gently onto my cheek, I feel its weight. It's not just a dot; it's a symbol, a shield. A shield from the evil eye, from harm, from the unknown that awaits. My mother's fingers linger for a moment as if holding on to me for just a little longer. I look at her, and I see the love in her eyes, the silent prayer.

"The black dot, a mother's plea,
To shield me, protect, and set me free.
Like Kali's strength, it guards my way,
Through every trial, come what may."

I think of Kali, the fierce protector, the goddess who shields her children with her divine strength. I feel her presence now, in this moment. The black dot is not just a mark on my skin; it is the love and protection of my mother, passed down from one generation to the next. It is a reminder that, no matter where life takes me, I am never alone.

Once the dot is placed, I feel a quiet calm settle over me. My mother steps back, her eyes misty but filled with pride. She looks at me, her hands resting on my shoulders, and for the first time today, I realize that I'm ready. Ready to become a bride. Ready to step into this new life, carrying the strength of my family, the love of my ancestors, and the blessings of the gods.

As I look into the mirror once more, I see a reflection that is both familiar and strange. The yellow thread, the black dot, the jasmine in my hair—these are all part of a ritual, yes, but they are also a part of me now. They mark me, not just as a bride, but as a woman who is tied to her past, to her roots, and to a future that is just beginning.

"In this mirror, I see my grace,
A bride, a daughter, in time and space.
With each thread, with each flower,
I step into my sacred hour."

And so, with every strand of jasmine, with every thread of yellow, and with every dot of protection, I step forward into the unknown. A bride, yes, but more than that—a daughter of tradition, a woman carrying the love and prayers of generations past, ready to embrace the sacred journey ahead.

There's something about this moment that makes me feel as if I'm being woven into the very fabric of tradition. The colors of the saree, the gold adorning me, the jewelry I've worn since I was a child—all are symbols, all are binding me to this role I'm about to take on. But none of it feels real.

A soft knock at the door. It's my father. His face is etched with the same blend of joy and sorrow I feel deep within me. I look up at him and find that his eyes, too, are glossy with unshed tears. This is the moment where he gives me away, and in his eyes, I can see the weight of all the memories we've shared.

"You look stunning, Anu," Mommy whispered from the back, her voice trembling. "Arjun won't be able to take his eyes off you."

I smiled faintly, but her words stirred a pang of doubt within me. Would he? In the weeks leading up to this day, Arjun's silence had been deafening. He had agreed to this marriage, yes, but he hadn't expressed much else. Still, I had convinced myself that it was nerves or perhaps the weight of familial expectations. After all, wasn't I nervous too?

"Dreams dressed in crimson hopes sewn with gold,
A story of love, waiting to unfold.
Yet silence whispers what hearts do not say,
Is love a promise, or does it drift away?"

When I arrived at the wedding venue, I felt the collective gaze of hundreds of guests settle on me. The hall was breathtaking, a perfect blend of tradition and elegance, with shimmering golden drapes, vibrant marigold decorations, and the gentle glow of oil lamps. The music of the *nadaswaram* and the rhythmic beat of the *mridangam* filled the air, setting the tone for the auspicious occasion. But I barely noticed any of it. My focus was on Arjun. As I walked towards the *mandap*, our eyes met. For a moment, I thought I saw something—a flicker of reassurance, maybe even affection. It was enough to quiet my fears, if only for a while.

The rituals unfolded in a blur. The chanting of mantras, the warmth of the sacred fire, the sound of my mother's quiet sobs as she placed my hand in Arjun's—it all felt like a dream. And when Arjun tied the *mangalsutra* around my neck, I thought, *This is it. Our story begins here.*

The reception was a grand affair, filled with laughter, music, and endless well-wishes. Sitting beside Arjun on the stage, I felt the first stirrings of hope. His occasional glances, and the way he brushed my hand as he reached for something, made me believe that perhaps we could build something beautiful together.

By the time the night wound down, I was both exhilarated and exhausted. The guests left one by one, and soon it was just the two of us. I was led to our room, a space meticulously decorated with fragrant flowers and warm candlelight. My heart raced as I sat on the edge of the bed, waiting for Arjun.

When he finally walked in, my breath caught. He looked calm, almost serene, but his eyes betrayed him. There was something in them—hesitation, maybe even sadness—that set my nerves on edge.

"Ananya," he began, his voice softer than I had ever heard it. "I need to tell you something."

My smile faltered. "What is it, Arjun?"

He sat down, his movements deliberate, as though every step he took brought him closer to something unbearable. "You've always been a part of my life," he said, his voice heavy. "We've grown up together and shared so many memories. I've always cared for you, but..."

His words hung in the air like a thundercloud, and my heart began to race. "But what, Arjun?" I asked, my voice trembling.

"I don't love you, Ananya," he said finally, the weight of his confession crashing into me like a tidal wave.

"The fire of love, now a fading ember,
Dreams of forever, I'll always remember.
But truth cuts sharper than any blade,
A story of silence, in shadows it's laid."

The room spun. I gripped the edge of the bed, trying to steady myself. "You don't...?" I whispered, the words barely audible over the sound of my heart-shattering.

"I never did," he admitted, his eyes glistening. "I agreed to this marriage because of my father. He wanted this union so much, wanted to reunite our families. I couldn't refuse him. I thought... I thought I could make it work, but I can't lie to you anymore."

Each word felt like a knife, cutting deeper than the last. Tears blurred my vision as I stared at him, my mind struggling to make sense of his confession. "Why didn't you tell me?" I asked, my voice breaking. "Why did you let me dream of a life with you if you never wanted this?"

His hands clenched, and he looked away. "Because I was afraid. Afraid of disappointing my father, of breaking his heart. And... there's something else."

I didn't think it was possible to feel more pain, but his hesitation sent a chill down my spine. "What else?" I demanded, my voice sharper now.

"In Australia… I met someone. Her name is Ramya," he said, his voice barely above a whisper. "I fell in love with her."

"A name that stings, a shadow of light,
Love found elsewhere, on a distant flight.
My heart, a fortress now left to decay,
Bound by a bond that will never stay."

The name hit me like a blow. I gasped, the air leaving my lungs as I tried to process what he was saying. "Ramya?" I repeated, the word foreign and bitter on my tongue. "You're in love with someone else?"

He nodded, his face a mask of guilt and regret. "I never wanted to hurt you, Ananya. I care about you, I do, but not the way you deserve. Not the way I care for her."

I stood, my legs trembling as if the ground beneath me had disappeared. "You've destroyed me, Arjun," I said, my voice shaking with rage and heartbreak. "You've ruined everything I've ever hoped for. And now I'm trapped in this marriage, bound to someone who doesn't even want me."

"A bride of dreams, now veiled in despair,
A love once imagined, dissolved in thin air.
Yet even in ruins, I'll find my way,
For broken hearts still see the light of day."

At that moment, I realized that the love I had nurtured for years had been one-sided, a story I had written alone. The man I thought would be my partner, my everything, had given his heart to someone else.

And now, I was left with nothing but a hollow promise of friendship and the bitter truth that our marriage was nothing more than a compromise.

As I stood there, the weight of everything pressing down on me, I could feel the tension crackling in the air. The silence stretched between us, but I couldn't hold it in anymore.

"Arjun, I don't even know who you are anymore," I said, my voice a mixture of hurt and anger. "You've spent all this time pretending, hiding your feelings, while I was here, thinking we had a future together. You could have said something—anything—to make me understand, but no. You let me walk down this path, expecting me to believe in a love that never existed."

He didn't move, his gaze fixed on me, but there was no apology in his eyes. There was no guilt. Only frustration. "You think I don't know that? Do you think I won't regret this? But I didn't have a choice, Ananya."

"Didn't have a choice?" I repeated, the words stinging. "You think I had a choice in this? Do you think it was my choice to marry you, to step into a life that was built on a lie? You could've said no. You could've stopped this at any point, but you chose not to. And now, you stand here, frustrated because you've ruined your own life. You're angry because you're stuck in this marriage, but it's *your* doing, Arjun."

He clenched his fists, his frustration bubbling over. "You don't get it. You don't understand how hard this has been for me. Do you think I wanted this? Do you think I wanted to marry someone I didn't love? I've been forced into this. And now I'm stuck with the mess I created, but that doesn't change the fact that there's someone else."

I felt my heart snap at his words. "Someone else?" I whispered, the bitter truth cutting through me. "You're in love with her, aren't you? The one you went to Australia for. Ramya. She's the one you wanted all along."

He looked at me, his expression a mix of frustration and sadness, but still no guilt. "Yes, I'm in love with her. But it's not that simple, Ananya. I didn't choose this. I didn't choose to hurt you, but I didn't have the guts to stop this either. Now, I'm stuck. And I'm supposed to pretend like I'm happy like I'm supposed to feel something for you when I don't. But that's the truth."

I shook my head in disbelief. "You let me think we had a future. You made me believe that we were building something together, Arjun. And now, you're telling me this is all a joke? That it's just a matter of convenience? That I'm just some... placeholder while you're pining away for someone else?"

"I didn't want this, Ananya," he said again, frustration boiling in his voice. "But I couldn't let my father down. I couldn't let anyone down, least of all you. And now look where we are. I'm stuck in this marriage, and you're here, hating me. I never wanted to hurt you like this."

I could feel the rage boiling inside me. "Don't you dare try to make this about your father? Don't you dare say that this is all for him? This is about you. About your cowardice. About the fact that you couldn't even stand up to your feelings, your own desires. You let me fall in love with you, Arjun. You *let* me believe that we had something special."

His voice rose, no longer trying to hide the edge of bitterness. "And now you're angry at me for not loving you the way you wanted. Well, maybe I never had a choice. Maybe I didn't want to hurt you, but the truth is, I couldn't give you what you needed. And I can't give you that now, no matter how much you want it."

The truth hit me like a slap. I felt the tears sting at the back of my eyes, but I held them back. "So, what now?" I asked, my voice cold, my words cutting through the space between us. "You want me to just accept this? To just pretend that everything is fine, that we're supposed to keep living in this charade? Is that it?"

His jaw tightened, his expression unreadable. "I don't know what you want from me, Ananya. I can't fix this. It's too far gone. Do you want to leave? Fine. Go. But don't act like this is all my fault. Don't act like you didn't know the truth somewhere deep down."

I took a step back, my heart heavy with the weight of his words. "No, Arjun. You're right. I did know. I knew that I was living in a dream, hoping that someday, you'd feel the same way. But now, I see it. We were never meant to be. Not like this. Not in a marriage where there was never any love from your side."

His eyes flickered with something—pain, maybe?—but he didn't say anything. He didn't try to stop me as I walked towards the door, my heart breaking with each step.

I turned to face him one last time, my voice soft but filled with finality. "I can't stay here, Arjun. I can't stay in a marriage that was built on silence, lies, and someone else's love. I deserve more than this. And so do you."

He didn't stop me. Didn't try to hold me back. He stood there, staring at me, frustration still etched on his face, but something else in his eyes—a quiet, unspoken regret.

I walked out of the room, leaving behind a life that never truly existed, and stepping into an uncertain future. But at least it would be mine.

"A love once promised, now shattered in pain,

A heart once hopeful, is now broken by blame.
In silence, we parted, with nothing to say,
Two souls once bound, now drifting away."

SHATTERED BOND

The door clicked shut behind me, sealing off a room I no longer recognized, a life I couldn't comprehend. The words Arjun had spoken the previous night reverberated in my mind, tearing at the fragile threads of hope I had clung to. I had walked away, leaving behind not just his indifference but also the unspoken realization that I was fighting a losing battle.

Morning came, but the weight in my chest hadn't lessened. The light streaming through the window felt foreign as if even the sun was mocking me. I stayed in the guest room, unsure of how to face him again, unsure if I even wanted to. But life doesn't pause for heartbreak.

When I finally emerged, I found him in the kitchen. He stood by the counter, drinking coffee, his posture stiff and unwelcoming. For a moment, I hesitated. Perhaps it would be easier to stay silent, to avoid confrontation, but the storm brewing inside me wouldn't let me.

"Arjun," I said, my voice strained but steady.

He didn't look at me. "What is it?" he asked, his tone flat, devoid of warmth or curiosity.

I walked closer, my arms crossed tightly over my chest. "We can't keep pretending this is normal. Last night... we need to talk about it."

Finally, he turned to face me, but his expression was unreadable, his eyes cold and detached. "What's there to talk about, Ananya? I told you the truth. Isn't that what you wanted?"

I flinched at his bluntness but pressed on. "No, Arjun. What I wanted was a marriage built on honesty, not silence. What I wanted was a partner who could meet me halfway, not someone who shuts me out and refuses to even try."

He set the cup down with deliberate slowness, the clink of ceramic against granite echoing in the room. "What exactly do you expect me to say? That I'll wake up tomorrow and suddenly fall in love with you? That I'll forget everything I feel for Ramya and pretend this is the life I wanted?"

"I'm not asking you to pretend," I snapped, anger flaring. "I'm asking you to let go of the past and give this marriage a chance. Is that really so impossible for you?"

He let out a bitter laugh, shaking his head. "You don't get it, do you? This isn't about choice, Ananya. This is about reality. I can't just erase my feelings because it's convenient for you."

"Convenient?" The word stung, and I felt my temper boil over. "Do you think this is convenient for me? Do you think I enjoy waking up every day knowing my husband is in love with someone else? That every smile, every glance, every touch from you is forced?"

"I never asked you to stay," he said coldly, his voice cutting like ice. "If you're so unhappy, you're free to leave."

The air was sucked from the room, his words a brutal slap. "That's how little I mean to you, isn't it?" I whispered. "You'd rather push me away than even try to make this work."

"You deserve better," he said, his voice quieter now but no less firm. "And I can't give you that. I won't pretend otherwise."

"But you can fight for her, right?" I challenged, my voice rising. "You can hold onto the idea of Ramya, cling to a dream that's long gone, but when it comes to me—to us—you won't even lift a finger."

He looked away, his jaw tightening. "This isn't about Ramya."

"Then what is it about, Arjun?" I demanded. "Because from where I'm standing, it seems like you've already decided this marriage means nothing to you."

He exhaled sharply, running a hand through his hair. "I didn't ask for this marriage, Ananya. I didn't choose you."

The words hit me like a blow, and I staggered under their weight. "I didn't choose you either, Arjun," I shot back, my voice trembling. "But I was willing to try. I was willing to put my heart on the line for us. Can you honestly say the same?"

His silence was answer enough.

"You can't, can you?" I said bitterly, my voice breaking. "Because you never even gave this a chance. From the moment we got married, you decided it was doomed. And now, you're using that as an excuse to push me away."

"Ananya," he said sharply, his tone laced with frustration. "Enough."

"No," I said firmly, stepping closer. "You don't get to shut me out like this. You don't get to treat me like I'm some unwelcome guest in my own marriage. If you can't love me, fine. But don't act like I'm the one who gave up."

His gaze met mine then, cold and unyielding. "I didn't ask for your love. I didn't ask for your sacrifice. So stop expecting something from me that I can't give."

The finality in his voice shattered something inside me. I took a step back, my chest heaving as I fought to keep the tears at bay. "You're right," I said quietly. "You didn't ask for my love. But you have it anyway. And that's the difference between us, Arjun. I was willing to give, even when you weren't. But I can't keep doing this alone."

He didn't respond, his silence louder than any words he could have spoken.

I turned and left the room, my footsteps echoing in the empty house. The distance between us wasn't just emotional anymore; it was palpable, a chasm that neither of us seemed willing—or able—to bridge.

For the first time, I realized that love, no matter how strong, couldn't survive without effort. And Arjun had made it clear—he had none left to give.

"Bound by vows, yet worlds apart,
A shattered bond, a wounded heart.
In the silence, the truth takes its toll,
Two fractured souls, seeking to be whole."

The days had slipped by in a haze of silence, the weight of unresolved emotions thickening the air between us. Arjun had retreated further into himself, his interactions with me reduced to strained, necessary exchanges. I had tried to adjust to this cold distance, forcing myself to accept that our marriage was nothing more than a painful arrangement. But nothing could have prepared me for what was to come.

One morning, the serenity of the house shattered. The sun had barely risen, casting a pale, golden light through the windows, when I heard a crash from the hallway. I rushed out, heart pounding, to find Arjun's father, my father-in-law collapsed on the floor. His face was pale, his hand clutching his chest as his breaths came in short, labored gasps.

"Arjun! Mounika Aunty!" I screamed, my voice frantic as I knelt beside him. "Appa, can you hear me? Hold on, we're getting help."

Arjun appeared in seconds, his face ashen as he took in the scene. "Appa!" he shouted, falling to his knees. "What happened?"

"I think it's a heart attack," I managed to say, my voice trembling.

Without wasting a moment, Arjun called for an ambulance. Time seemed to stretch endlessly as we waited, every second punctuated by the sound of his father's ragged breathing. I held his hand, whispering words of comfort, though I wasn't sure if he could hear me.

The paramedics arrived and swiftly took over. Arjun and I followed the ambulance to the hospital, the ride heavy with unspoken fears. Mounika Aunty sat silently beside me, her hands trembling as she clutched her saree pallu. Her face was etched with worry, her eyes reflecting the turmoil within.

In the hospital, the doctors worked tirelessly, but their expressions told us what we dreaded to hear. Hours passed, and the waiting room became a prison of anxiety. Arjun paced the room, his fists clenched, his face a mask of anguish. I wanted to comfort him, to tell him everything would be okay, but I knew my words would sound hollow.

Finally, a doctor approached us. His expression was somber. "We did everything we could," he said softly. "But his heart was too weak. I'm so sorry."

The words hit like a thunderclap. Mounika Aunty let out a wail, collapsing into a chair. Arjun stood frozen, his face pale, his eyes wide with disbelief. I reached out to touch his arm, but he pulled away sharply.

"This is your fault," he said, his voice trembling with suppressed rage. His words struck me like a physical blow.

"What?" I whispered, unable to process what he had just said.

"You came into this house, into my life, and everything started falling apart," he spat, his voice rising. "If it weren't for you, none of this would have happened. Appa would still be alive."

The weight of his accusation was unbearable. Tears welled up in my eyes, but I refused to let them fall. "Arjun, how can you say that? I did nothing but care for him, for all of you."

He didn't respond, his gaze fixed on some distant point. His silence spoke louder than any words ever could.

Over the next few days, the house was engulfed in grief. Relatives and friends came to pay their respects, their voices hushed, their expressions solemn. Mounika Aunty was inconsolable, her cries echoing through the hallways. I tried to be there for her, to offer her some comfort, but she barely acknowledged my presence.

Arjun, on the other hand, had become a ghost of himself.

He avoided me entirely, his coldness more pronounced than ever. The few times we crossed paths, he wouldn't even look at me. The blame he placed on me hung in the air, unspoken yet palpable.

One evening, I found him in his father's study, staring at a photograph of his parents. His face was a mask of pain and guilt. I hesitated at the door, unsure if I should approach him.

"Arjun," I began softly.

"What do you want?" he asked, his voice devoid of emotion.

"I... I just wanted to see if you're okay."

He turned to face me, his eyes filled with a mixture of anger and sadness. "Do I look okay, Ananya? My father is gone. The one person who held this family together is gone. And now... everything is falling apart."

I took a step closer. "I know you're hurting, Arjun. I am too. But blaming me won't bring him back."

His laugh was bitter. "You don't get it, do you? You were the final straw. Appa fought for this marriage, for you to be here, despite everything. And now he's gone. I can't help but wonder if... things would've been different if none of this had happened."

Tears streamed down my face. "I didn't ask for this, Arjun. I didn't ask to be here, in this marriage, in this house. But I'm trying. I've been trying, even when you've done nothing but push me away."

"Well, maybe you should stop trying," he snapped. "Because this... us... it's not working. It never will."

His words shattered whatever fragile hope I had left. I turned and walked away, my heart heavy with the weight of his rejection.

In the days that followed, the cold war between us deepened. We lived like strangers under the same roof, bound by the invisible chains of duty and grief. Arjun's blame hung over me like a dark cloud, a constant reminder of how far apart we had drifted.

Mounika Aunty, too, withdrew into herself, her grief consuming her. The house, once filled with laughter and warmth, now felt like a mausoleum, a place where happiness had been buried alongside Arjun's father. And in the midst of it all, I was left to navigate a life that felt more like a punishment than a partnership.

"In grief's shadow, love turns cold,
Words unspoken, stories untold.
Blame and silence, hearts astray,
A house of sorrow, where dreams decay."

Unveiled Secrets

I thought of letting Ramya know about this and let both of them have a good life together. It took me hours to summon the courage to dial her number. I stared at my phone, my fingers trembling as I pressed the call button. The name "Ramya" on the screen felt heavier than it should have. I had rehearsed the conversation countless times in my head, but as the dial tone buzzed in my ear, my mind went blank.

"Hello?" her voice came through, calm and unsuspecting.

"Hi... is this Ramya?" I asked, my voice wavering slightly.

"Yes, who's this?"

I took a deep breath. "My name is Ananya. I'm calling about Arjun."

There was a pause, and I could sense her confusion. "About Arjun? What is this about?"

"I think it's best if we meet and talk in person," I said, trying to keep my tone neutral. "It's important."

She hesitated, and I could almost hear her thoughts racing. "Why should I meet you? What do you have to do with Arjun?"

"I promise I'll explain everything when we meet," I said, my heart pounding. "Please. It won't take much of your time."

Her silence stretched on, and I wondered if she would hang up. Then, she said, "Fine. Where?"

We agreed on a small café near her office. She didn't sound angry or accusatory—just curious. She didn't know who I was yet, and that made it easier for me to keep going.

When I arrived at the café, she was already there, seated by the window with a cup of coffee in her hand. Her expression was composed, though I could see hints of curiosity in her eyes as I approached.

"You're Ananya?" she asked when I stood before her.

"Yes," I said, taking a seat. "Thank you for meeting me."

She nodded, her gaze sharp. "So, what is this about? How do you know Arjun?"

Her question hung in the air, and I realized this was the moment of truth. "I... I was married to him," I said softly.

Her eyes widened, her calm demeanor shattering instantly. "What? Married?"

I nodded, forcing myself to meet her gaze. "Yes. We're in the process of getting divorced."

"Divorced?" she repeated, her voice rising. "Are you out of your mind? Why would you—what happened?"

I tried to explain, my words careful and measured. "Ramya, sometimes two people just aren't right for each other. I gave it everything I had, but—"

"Don't give me that!" she snapped, cutting me off. "Do you even understand what you're saying? Divorce? That's not something you throw around lightly. Do you know what this will do to him?"

I swallowed hard. "I know it's not easy, but this is what's best for both of us. The hearing is in a few days."

Her face contorted with disbelief. "A few days? Are you serious? And you're just telling me now? How could you even let it get to this point?"

"It wasn't an easy decision," I said, my voice trembling. "I've thought about this for months."

"Then think about it again," she shot back. "Withdraw it. Fix this. Do you even care about him?"

"I care about him enough to let him go," I said quietly.

Ramya let out a bitter laugh. "Let him go? That's just an excuse for giving up. Marriage isn't something you just walk away from, Ananya. You fight for it!"

"I did fight," I said, my voice breaking. "But sometimes, fighting just makes things worse."

She shook her head, her expression hardening. "You're making a mistake. A huge mistake. And I'll tell him that too."

"Ramya, I called you because I wanted you to know the truth, not to justify myself," I said, trying to stay calm. "I didn't expect you to understand, but this is my decision."

Her eyes blazed with anger. "You're right. I don't understand. And I don't think I ever will."

Without another word, she stood up, grabbing her bag. "I

hope you realize what you're doing before it's too late."

She stormed out, leaving me sitting there with a lump in my throat.

Later, I learned she confronted Arjun, her fury turning into silence when he defended my decision. Eventually, she stopped speaking to him altogether. It wasn't the outcome I'd hoped for, but it was the one I had to accept.

As I sat in my room, the weight of my situation felt unbearable. I had no one to turn to, no one to help me make sense of all this confusion. But then, through the haze of panic and uncertainty, a thought crossed my mind: RJ Kabir. He had been my anchor once, the one person who had helped me find my voice, who had encouraged me to stand up for myself when I thought I was too weak to do so.

Kabir had been my confidant during some of the darkest moments of my life. His words always had a way of cutting through the noise in my mind, bringing clarity when I needed it the most. And so, without thinking twice, I grabbed my phone and dialed his number.

The call connected after a few rings, and his familiar voice was a balm to my frayed nerves.

"Ananya, hey! How are you?" Kabir's voice was warm, but I could sense the hesitation in my silence.

"I... Kabir, I need to talk," I said, my voice trembling despite my best efforts to stay calm. "I don't know where to start. Things are... complicated."

There was a pause on the other end. "What's going on?" Kabir asked, his tone shifting to one of concern.

I took a deep breath and let it all spill out. The divorce, the betrayal, the anger, the heartbreak—and then the revelation that I was pregnant. The weight of it all came rushing out in a flood of words, and by the time I finished speaking, I felt empty, like the air had been sucked out of me.

Kabir listened patiently, never interrupting. When I finally fell silent, he let out a slow breath. "Ananya," he said quietly, "I'm really sorry you're going through this. But I need to ask you something—have you told anyone in your family about this? Your mother? Your in-laws?"

The question took me off guard, and for a moment, I didn't know how to respond.

"I... no," I said, feeling a pang of guilt in my chest. "I haven't told anyone. Not about the divorce, not about the pregnancy. I didn't want to worry them. I thought I could handle it on my own. I didn't want them to judge me."

Kabir's voice hardened, a trace of anger creeping in. "Ananya, this isn't something you should be handling alone. You have family, people who care about you. Especially your mother and your mother-in-law. You can't keep everything bottled up, especially something like this."

I could feel his frustration through the phone, his words cutting through the fog of my own doubts. "You've been strong, I know. But now, you need to be strong enough to share this with the people who matter. They're your support system, Ananya. You can't carry this burden on your own."

I swallowed hard, feeling my chest tighten. His words made sense, but the thought of confronting my family, of telling them the truth, terrified me.

"I don't know if I can, Kabir," I admitted, my voice barely a whisper. "What if they're disappointed in me? What if they think I failed?"

Kabir's response was immediate, his voice softening. "You're not a failure, Ananya. You're just a woman trying to find her way through an incredibly tough situation. And you deserve the support, the understanding, and the love of the people around you. Don't rob yourself of that just because you're scared of their reaction. You'll never know how they'll respond unless you give them the chance to be there for you."

I sat there, his words reverberating in my mind, and for the first time in weeks, I felt a flicker of hope. Maybe Kabir was right. Maybe it was time to stop pretending I could handle everything alone.

"I'll do it," I said, a resolve settling over me. "I'll tell them. I'll start with my mom. She deserves to know."

Kabir's tone softened again, and I could hear the relief in his voice. "Good. And remember, I'm always here if you need to talk. You don't have to face this alone."

I hung up the phone with a sense of determination building within me. It wasn't going to be easy, but I knew I had to take that step. I had to be honest with the people who loved me, especially my mother, who had always stood by me. The weight of my decisions was heavy, but for the first time in a long while, I felt a glimmer of control.

As I prepared myself for the difficult conversations ahead, I realized that Kabir's words were more than just advice. They were a lifeline. And I was finally ready to take hold of it.

I knew my mother had always been a woman of strength, but I also knew she had a heart that wore her vulnerabilities openly. I didn't want to see her hurt, and yet, I couldn't avoid the truth any longer. I took a deep breath, wiping away the cold sweat that had formed on my palms, and dialed her number.

"Hello, Ananya," her voice came through the line, gentle but filled with warmth. "How are you, beta?"

"Hi, Amma," I said, my voice wavering despite my attempts to steady it. "I need to talk to you about something... something important."

There was a pause on the other end. I could feel her shift, sensing the seriousness in my tone. "What is it, beta? Is everything alright?"

I closed my eyes, struggling to hold back the tears that threatened to spill. "I... I don't know how to say this, but... Arjun and I—" I faltered, unsure how to go on. "Things aren't the way they should be, Amma. We're... we're not happy. I'm filing for a divorce."

There was a heavy silence on the other end, and for a moment, I thought the call had disconnected. My heart pounded as I waited for her response.

"You... you're getting a divorce?" Her voice cracked, and I could hear the shock in her words. "But why, Ananya? What happened?"

The floodgates opened, and I found myself spilling the truth in a rush. I told her about the constant emotional neglect, Arjun's behavior, the betrayal I had felt, and the hurt that had built up inside me over the past six months. But I left out the details of my pregnancy, unsure if I was ready to share that part of me.

"Amma, it's just... I don't see a way out of this marriage," I said, my voice choking on the final words. "I can't do this anymore."

There was a long silence after that, one so heavy that it felt as if time itself had stopped. I held my breath, waiting, praying for her to say something—anything.

And then, I heard it.

"Ananya," her voice came through, shaky and weak. "I... I need to sit down."

Before I could respond, the line went dead. My heart skipped a beat. I immediately tried calling her back, but it went straight to voicemail. Panic surged through me as I frantically dialed again, my hands trembling.

I could feel the air around me closing in, suffocating me with the dread of what was unfolding.

Minutes passed, but it felt like hours. Finally, I received a call, but it wasn't from my mother. It was from my uncle, who lived nearby.

"Ananya, beta, you need to come to the hospital right now," he said, his voice urgent. "Your mother... she collapsed. We're on our way to the ER."

My chest tightened a wave of fear and guilt crashing over me. I had never wanted this for her. I hadn't meant to cause her this much pain. But in my selfish pursuit of escaping a life that was no longer mine, I had unknowingly pushed her to her breaking point.

I rushed to the hospital, my mind in a haze, my heart heavy with regret. When I arrived, I found my mother lying in a hospital bed, pale and weak, hooked up to an IV. My uncle was sitting beside her, his face etched with worry.

"She's stable for now," he said quietly as I stood at the doorway, unable to move closer. "But the doctors say it's a result of the stress. Ananya, you have to be more careful. This is too much for her."

I nodded numbly, my throat tight as I fought back the tears. I had done this. I had caused this. In my bid to gain control over my own life, I had shattered my mother's.

I sat by her side, taking her hand in mine, and whispered an apology. "I'm so sorry, Amma. I never meant for you to get hurt. Please forgive me. I didn't know what else to do."

My mother stirred slightly, her eyes fluttering open. She looked at me, and there was a moment of recognition before the pain flashed in her eyes. "Ananya," she whispered, her voice hoarse. "What have you done? What's happening... why didn't you tell me?"

"I didn't want to worry you, Amma," I said, my voice cracking. "I thought I could handle it. I thought I could fix things on my own."

Her hand squeezed mine weakly. "Ananya, you're my daughter. You don't have to go through this alone. I'm here for you. Always."

But her words were weak, and I could see the toll that my silence had taken on her. It was too late for regrets, but I had learned a painful lesson. In trying to protect my family from the truth, I had only hurt them more.

The hospital room was quiet, the only sound being the steady beep of the monitor next to my mother's bed. She lay there, pale and fragile, her hand gripping mine with a weak but firm hold. The worry on her face was apparent, but the silence between us was heavier than I could bear. I wanted to tell her everything, all the pain, all the fear that had been building inside me for months, but I didn't know where to begin.

The door creaked open, and my family began trickling into the room, one by one. My father entered first, his face lined with concern as he moved to my mother's side. Then came my aunt, her voice immediately scolding me for not telling her about my troubles sooner. And finally, Aunt Mounika—Arjun's mother, who was always kind but had no idea of the storm that had been brewing in my life.

Aunt Mounika's expression softened when she saw my mother, and she immediately went to her, brushing her hair gently. "Don't worry, Latha," she whispered. "Everything will be okay."

I stayed quiet in the corner of the room, my eyes downcast, still unsure of how to share the truth that had been weighing on me. I couldn't keep hiding it any longer, but my heart pounded with the fear of how they would react.

It wasn't until my father turned to me with a serious expression that I realized it was time.

"Ananya," he said quietly, his voice laced with worry. "What's really going on? Your mother is devastated. You've been hiding something from us, haven't you?"

I felt my stomach tighten as I stared at my mother, who was watching me with tired, understanding eyes. She deserved the truth. I owed it to her, to all of them.

"I... I've applied for a divorce," I said softly, my voice trembling.

The room went completely silent, and for a long moment, no one spoke. My father's face shifted from concern to shock. "From Arjun?" he asked, his voice full of disbelief.

I nodded, barely able to meet his gaze. "Yes. We're not

happy. It's been six months... of misery. I can't live like this anymore, Papa."

The weight of those words hung in the air, and my father took a step toward me, his face tightening. "Why didn't you tell us sooner, Ananya? Why keep this from us?"

"I didn't want to burden you," I whispered, feeling the sting of guilt cut through me. "I thought I could handle it. But I couldn't. I've been hiding it from everyone, even myself."

Aunt Mounika, who had been standing silently by the bed, now stepped forward, her face filled with confusion and concern. "What do you mean? You applied for divorce from my son?"

I nodded again, swallowing hard. "Yes. It's not just the marriage. There's so much more. And... I'm pregnant, Aunt Mounika. I'm pregnant with Arjun's child."

The words felt foreign on my lips, but I couldn't stop them now. The silence in the room deepened as Aunt Mounika stood frozen in shock.

"You're pregnant?" she repeated, her voice faint.

I looked at her, my own heart aching. "Yes. And I don't know what to do. I didn't want to go through this alone, but now I don't know where to turn."

Aunt Mounika took a slow step back, her face pale. "Oh my God... how did this happen? Why didn't you tell us sooner?"

I felt the weight of her words, of everyone's shock, pressing down on me. I had kept it all inside, thinking I could handle it alone, but now the truth was out, and it felt like everything I had tried to avoid was crashing down on me.

My father's expression softened, and he stepped closer to me, placing a hand on my shoulder. "You don't have to do this by yourself, Ananya. We're your family. We're here for you, no matter what."

But my heart was still heavy, burdened by the decisions I had made. I had already filed for divorce, but now this new reality, the pregnancy, had added another layer of uncertainty to my already complicated life.

Aunt Mounika, still processing everything, turned to my father. "We need to talk, all of us. This is too much to deal with right now."

My aunt, who had been silent until now, nodded in agreement. "She's right. We need to get to the bottom of this. Ananya, we need to understand what happened. We need to figure out how we can help."

I nodded, the weight of it all beginning to feel more bearable with every word spoken, every bit of support I felt from my family. I had been afraid of their judgment, of their disappointment, but instead, I was finding understanding

As they continued to discuss what to do next, my thoughts wandered back to the moment when I decided to take this step, to finally file for divorce. I had never imagined that it would lead to this—pregnant, divorced, uncertain of my future.

But I wasn't alone anymore. I had my family. And maybe, just maybe, I could figure out how to rebuild my life from here.

A Chance to Breathe

Back in my aunt's house, The tension in the air was thick, the kind that makes it hard to breathe. My heart filled with grief and vexed with Arjun's behavior. As I sat in front of Mounika Aunty's sharp gaze. I had expected her to be upset, but nothing prepared me for the torrent of emotions that followed.

"You should have told me, Ananya," Mounika Aunty's voice was trembling with anger, yet there was an underlying concern I couldn't ignore. "I could've helped. I could've made things right. But instead, you just went ahead with this divorce nonsense without even telling me what was really going on!" Her eyes were filled with hurt and confusion, and I could feel the weight of her words pressing down on me.

I couldn't meet her eyes. I knew she was right, that I should have confided in her, that I should have shared the pain I was going through. But I had kept it all to myself, trying to protect everyone from the heartbreak I was feeling. And now, everything was falling apart.

"Aunty, I didn't want this. I didn't want the divorce," I whispered, my voice barely above a breath. "But Arjun… his actions, the way he was distant, the way he didn't seem to care about me anymore… I couldn't take it. I tried, Aunty. I tried so hard. But it felt like he was slipping away from me.

I didn't know what else to do."

Mounika Aunty's face softened for a moment, but then her features tightened in frustration. "Ananya, I understand that things can get difficult, but you didn't give me a chance to help! You didn't give me a chance to speak to Arjun, to understand what was happening." She paused, taking a deep breath before continuing, "You should've trusted me. You should've come to me earlier."

I lowered my head, my hands twisting in my lap. Her words hit me like a storm, and I couldn't find a way to defend myself. I had kept my pain inside for so long, thinking I was protecting everyone, but now I was left feeling exposed and vulnerable.

But then, Mounika Aunty's gaze shifted from me to Arjun. I could feel the change in the air as she turned her anger on him.

"You!" She pointed a finger at him, her voice sharp. "How could you let things get this far? How could you treat Ananya like this? She's been nothing but good to you, and look at how you've treated her! You've pushed her into this, and now you're sitting there silent, not even taking responsibility for your actions!"

Arjun didn't flinch. He remained silent, his gaze averted, avoiding the storm in Mounika Aunty's eyes. It was like he was a shadow, fading further into the background as though he didn't even want to be part of this conversation. The lack of response only infuriated Mounika Aunty more.

"You think this is all on Ananya?" she continued, her voice rising in anger. "Do you have any idea how much you've hurt her? Do you realize the weight of your silence, your neglect? You're the reason she feels like this! You're the reason she's considering a divorce! And now you can't even speak up and defend your actions?" Her voice broke at the end, filled with a mixture of frustration and sorrow.

I could feel the walls between Arjun and me growing taller with each word she said. He hadn't even tried to fix things, hadn't even tried to explain himself. Instead, he just sat there, letting Mounika Aunty's scolding wash over him without so much as a murmur.

Mounika Aunty turned back to me, her face softening. "Ananya, I know you're hurt, but don't make this permanent. Don't let this decision define your life. You're too young, too full of potential to let one person's actions shape your future. If you want to fix this, if you truly want to give this marriage another chance, I'm here for you. But don't close that door forever. Not yet."

I swallowed hard, the words stinging in my throat. I didn't want the divorce, but what choice did I have? Arjun's indifference had shattered me, leaving me with nothing but the painful decision to walk away. But hearing Mounika Aunty's plea, I couldn't help but wonder if I had been too quick to give up and if there was still hope left.

Arjun remained silent, still refusing to take responsibility for what had happened. His silence was suffocating, like an invisible weight pressing down on me. How could he let me go through this alone? How could he not see the damage his actions had caused?

Mounika Aunty finally let out a sigh, looking between Arjun and me, her disappointment evident. "I just don't understand you, Arjun," she said softly, her voice tired. "I don't know who you've become, but I do know this—you've lost something precious, and I hope you realize it before it's too late."

With that, the room fell silent. The weight of Mounika

Aunty's words hung in the air, and I could feel the distance between Arjun and me growing wider with every passing second.

And in that silence, I realized something—maybe I wasn't the one who needed to fight for this relationship anymore. Maybe it was time for Arjun to step up and prove he still cared. But would he? Would he ever realize what he was losing before it was gone?

Here's a scene where Ananya speaks her last words to Arjun two days before the divorce hearing, trying to convince him to not go through with it, not for their marriage, but for the sake of their child. Arjun's behavior changes, and he cancels the divorce, though it takes time for him to fully accept Ananya as his soulmate.

It was two days before the hearing. My mind had been a battlefield for the past few weeks, filled with endless thoughts of regret, heartbreak, and uncertainty. The decision to go through with the divorce had torn me apart, but in my heart, I knew I couldn't keep holding onto something that was slipping through my fingers like sand.

But then… there was the child. The life growing inside me. And though my marriage was on the brink of shattering, I knew that the child deserved better. Deserved more than the broken pieces of a relationship.

I stood there in front of him, my hands trembling, unsure of how to say what I had been thinking for days. Arjun was sitting on the edge of the sofa, his eyes tired, distant—still the same man who had driven me to this decision.

"Arjun, I… I've been thinking a lot these past few days," I began, my voice soft but firm, "and I've come to a conclusion."

He didn't respond right away. I wasn't sure if he even heard me, but I continued, determined to speak my heart.

"We've been through so much," I said, trying to hold back the tears that threatened to break free. "And I know we've both made mistakes. I know I've hurt you, and maybe I'm the reason things started falling apart. But please, listen to me now... this isn't just about you and me anymore."

Arjun turned his head to meet my gaze, his expression unreadable. But something in his eyes, a flicker of recognition, made me push forward.

"For the sake of the child, Arjun," I whispered, my voice breaking, "can't we at least stay together as parents? We don't need to be husband and wife. We don't need to go back to what we once were. But for the sake of the life growing inside me, can we put aside our differences and just... be there for this child? Can we raise them together, even if it's just as a family, not a married couple?"

The silence stretched between us. Arjun remained motionless, his gaze intense, his jaw clenched. I could feel the weight of my words settling in the room, hanging there like an unspoken plea. I wasn't asking for his love. I wasn't asking for a miracle. I was simply asking for him to be a father, to give our children what they deserved—a chance at a loving home.

Arjun finally broke the silence, his voice low, almost a whisper. "Ananya..." He sighed deeply, his eyes falling to the floor. "I don't know if I can do this. After everything, I don't know if I can just... pretend like everything is fine."

I felt my heart drop. He still didn't understand, did he? He still couldn't see that this wasn't about us anymore. It wasn't about fixing a broken marriage. It was about the future, about a child who would need both of us, whether we were together or not.

"Arjun," I said, my voice desperate now, "I'm not asking for us to fix everything. I'm not asking for the kind of love we once had. But for the child, we need to be there, at least for them. Please don't let this divorce happen. For their sake… for our sake, let's try. Let's just try to make it work in a way that we can both accept."

There was a long pause. Arjun stared at the ground, his fists clenched tightly. I could see the internal battle playing out in his mind, and for a brief moment, I thought he might walk away again, just like he always did.

But then, he finally spoke. His voice was quieter now, as though the anger had left him, replaced by something more vulnerable.

"You're right, Ananya," he said, his voice strained. "I've been selfish. I've been so focused on my own pain and confusion that I didn't even consider what you were going through, what we're going through. I wasn't there for you. I wasn't there for the child."

I nodded my heart racing, the hope that had been buried deep inside me flickering to life again.

"I don't know if I can be the husband you wanted, or the man you needed," Arjun continued, his eyes finally meeting mine. "But I can be there for our child. I can put aside everything else, and I can do my part. If you'll have me… I'll stay. I'll cancel the divorce."

I didn't know what to say at first. The words I had longed to hear, the ones I had hoped for in vain, were now before me. Arjun, the man who had distanced himself so completely, was finally acknowledging his responsibilities. But it didn't feel like a victory. It didn't feel like everything was magically fixed.

"Thank you," I said softly, my eyes welling up with tears. But the words felt hollow because I knew that this wasn't the end. It was the beginning of something uncertain, something fragile. Arjun wasn't ready to fully embrace the role I needed him to. But for the first time, he was willing to try.

"I'm not asking you to love me like you once did," I whispered, "But I need you to be there for us. I need you to show up, even if it's just for our child."

He nodded slowly, his gaze distant. "I can do that, Ananya," he said, though I could hear the hesitation in his voice. "But... it will take time. I don't know if I can accept everything yet. I don't know if I can look at you the same way again. But I'll be there, for the child. I'll try."

That was all I needed. He was trying. And for now, that was enough.

After the conversation, things didn't change overnight. Arjun and I weren't suddenly a perfect family, but there was a shift. A small one, but it was enough to make me feel like maybe, just maybe, we could get through this, for the child.

The first real sign that he was trying came when I fell ill one evening. It wasn't anything too serious, just a fever and weakness from the stress and exhaustion, but Arjun noticed. He was in the living room, absorbed in something, when I collapsed on the sofa, unable to stand up.

I had expected him to be indifferent, to just leave me to my own devices as he had before. But instead, I felt him at my side within moments, his hand on my forehead, his touch surprisingly gentle.

"Ananya," he said, his voice full of concern. "You're burning up. We need to get you to the hospital."

I blinked, still dazed from the fever. "No, it's just a cold. I'll be fine."

He didn't listen. Arjun helped me to my feet, guiding me toward the door. There was no anger in his eyes, no frustration, just a calm determination. He wasn't the same man who had walked out on me weeks ago.

We reached the hospital, and Arjun stayed by my side through every moment. He held my hand when the nurse took my blood pressure, sat in the waiting area as I rested, and even made sure I had everything I needed when the doctor gave me medication. It wasn't grand gestures; it was the small acts of kindness that spoke volumes to me.

I tried to push him away at first, trying to insist that he didn't need to care for me. But Arjun wouldn't have it. Every time I attempted to retreat into myself, he pulled me back—gently, patiently.

Once we were home, he made me soup and sat with me, silently keeping me company as I rested. His presence was comforting, and for the first time in a long while, I felt like I wasn't alone.

Days passed, and this new version of Arjun—this version that cared—became more apparent. I started noticing the little things. When I woke up in the morning, I found my tea already prepared, the way I liked it. He would bring me the paper in the mornings and check on me when I took a nap. And when I would become overwhelmed with the thought of the divorce hearing, he would sit next to me and hold my hand without a word, as though telling me, *I'm here with you.*

There were moments when I could feel the walls between us begin to crumble. One evening, as I sat on the balcony, staring out at the dark sky, I felt his presence beside me.

"I've been thinking," he said, his voice softer than usual. "About what you said. About being there for the child... about trying."

I turned to him, meeting his gaze. "And?"

Arjun hesitated for a moment, then slowly took a deep breath. "I'm not going to lie and say everything's perfect. I don't know if I can love you the way u wanted. But... I can't deny that I care for you. I care for you in a way I didn't understand before."

My heart skipped a beat, and I looked at him, unsure of how to respond.

"I think... I think I'm starting to understand you, Ananya," he continued, his voice still hesitant but steady. "I was so angry, so wrapped up in my own pain that I couldn't see how much you were hurting too. I was blind to everything you were going through. But now... now I see it. I see how much you love me. And I see how much you love this child."

I didn't know what to say. There was so much unspoken between us, so many things that still needed to be worked through. But hearing him admit that he was starting to understand, starting to acknowledge my love, made my heart swell.

"You've always been there for me, Ananya," he said, a soft smile tugging at his lips. "Even when I didn't deserve it. I want to be there for you now. I'm not perfect, and I'm still figuring things out. But I'm here. For you. And for us."

At that moment, I realized that maybe we weren't as far

apart as I had once thought. Maybe, just maybe, we could rebuild. It wouldn't be easy, and it wouldn't happen overnight, but I could see the man I once loved—broken and flawed, but willing to try.

The next few weeks felt different. Arjun continued to show me that he cared, little by little. He even started attending doctor's appointments with me, not out of obligation but because he wanted to be there. I couldn't deny that something had changed inside him. He was no longer the man who walked away when things got tough. He was the man who was showing up, day after day, trying to be better, trying to be there for me and our child.

But even then, I knew the road ahead was still uncertain. Arjun was trying, but he wasn't ready to accept me fully yet, not in the way I had hoped. He still struggled with his own feelings, with his past pain, and with the idea of us being more than just parents to our child.

But I had hope. And for the first time in a long time, I felt like we were on the path toward something better. It wouldn't be easy. It would take time, patience, and understanding. But I was willing to wait, for the sake of our child and for the possibility that, in time, Arjun could find his way back to me—not just as a father, but as a partner.

"In the silence between us, love started to speak,
Whispers of hope in the pain we both seek.
The cracks in our hearts began to mend,
A journey not of love, but the will to bend."

When Hope Finds a Way

The days following Arjun's confession were like walking through fog. The weight of uncertainty still loomed over us, but something had changed. The silence between us, which had been suffocating, had softened. There was a quiet tension now, a tentative hope, like the first rays of sunlight after a long storm.

"Between the dark and the dawn, a fragile light,
Unspoken words that take their flight,
In the quiet, we begin to heal,
Slow steps forward, hearts that feel."

Arjun wasn't perfect—far from it—but he was here. And that was more than I could have asked for, at least for now.

I woke up each morning to find him already awake, moving quietly around the house, taking care of things that used to be my responsibility. It was strange but comforting. His presence, though still distant in some ways, felt like a promise of something better. He made me breakfast one morning, something simple—a bowl of porridge with a cup of tea, just the way I liked it. I hadn't asked him to do any of this. He just did.

It wasn't grand gestures. It wasn't the romance I had once dreamed of, but it was something else. It was real. It was a man, flawed and struggling, but trying nonetheless.

"It's the little things that speak the most,
A soft touch when we need it most,
No grand gestures, no perfect rhyme,
Just being present, in this moment in time."

I watched him as he moved around the house, his brow furrowed in concentration as he worked on fixing a leaking faucet in the kitchen. I noticed how his hands, once so distant, now seemed to seek out mine in small, meaningful moments—when we sat together for meals when we watched the child's first ultrasound, or even when he just reached for my hand when the silence between us felt too heavy.

Yet, even though things were slowly improving, the walls between us were still there. Arjun had stepped up, but he had not yet fully embraced what it meant to be my partner again. We were both walking on a tightrope, afraid to fall, unsure of how to move forward.

"Walls between us, built so high,
Fading slowly, time passing by,
A tightrope walk, but hand in hand,
We find our way through shifting sand."

One evening, as the sun began to set, I found myself sitting on the balcony, staring out at the horizon. The colors in the sky were a mixture of orange, pink, and purple—a sight I once would have shared with Arjun, basking in the beauty of the world together. But tonight, I was alone with my thoughts, wondering what our future would look like.

And then, I felt him. He had come outside without a word, standing quietly behind me before 'he finally spoke.

"I'm not good at this," he said, his voice rough with vulnerability. "I don't know how to make everything right between us. I don't know how to be the husband you need or the man you deserve. But... I'm trying. I know it's not enough, but I want you to know that I'm here. I'm here for you and our child."

His words were simple, but they hit me hard. For the first time in a long while, I could feel the sincerity in his voice. It was no longer about him just saying the right things—it was about him *showing up*. He wasn't pretending everything was perfect. He wasn't pretending to be the man he wasn't. He was being honest, and that honesty was the first step toward healing.

I turned around to face him, meeting his gaze. His eyes were filled with regret, with longing, and with something else—something I hadn't seen in him for a long time. There was a flicker of the man I had once loved, the one who had stood by my side through thick and thin. But I knew that he wasn't there yet. He wasn't fully back. Not yet.

"I know it's hard, Arjun," I said softly. "It's not going to be easy for either of us. But we're in this together, for our child. And... maybe, just maybe, we can find a way to make it work."

He nodded, stepping closer to me. His presence, though still cautious, felt more genuine now. "I want that too, Ananya. I'm not perfect, and I know I can't undo everything. But I want to try. For you. For the baby. And for us."

The words hung in the air between us, fragile and uncertain, but for the first time, they didn't feel like empty promises. They felt like the beginning of something.

"The future's a road we walk unsure,
But together, we'll find a way to endure,
No perfect answers, no easy way,

But one step at a time, we'll find our way."

And so we stood there, on the balcony, not knowing what the future held but willing to take one small step forward together. It wasn't a promise of happily ever after. It wasn't a guarantee that things would magically fall into place. But it was a promise of effort, of trying. And sometimes, that's all we need.

We spent the following days in a quiet rhythm. Arjun continued to show up, bit by bit, in ways that mattered—taking responsibility for his actions, offering his support, and, most importantly, being present in ways he hadn't been before. It wasn't perfect, but it was progress.

And I—though still cautious, still unsure of what the future would bring—started to see that maybe this broken road could lead to something new. Something different. Something worth fighting for.

As the days passed, Arjun and I began to share more of our feelings—our hopes, our fears, our dreams. It wasn't always easy, and there were moments when the weight of the past threatened to break us. But through every tear, and every hard conversation, we started to rebuild. Slowly, cautiously, but with a quiet understanding that, for the sake of our child, we would try to make this work.

And in the stillness of those quiet nights, when the world seemed to stand still, I felt a flicker of hope. A hope that maybe, just maybe, we could find our way back to each other—not as the people we once were, but as the people we had become through all the pain and heartache.

For now, that was enough. A glimpse of something beautiful in the distance, waiting for us to take the next step toward it.

In the silence between us, love didn't speak in grand gestures, but in the small moments where we simply tried. And that was enough to keep going.

The day I had been dreading and eagerly anticipating arrived. The contractions started early in the morning, sharp and relentless. I had been counting down to this moment for months, but now that it was finally here, it felt surreal. Arjun was beside me, not saying much, but his presence was a silent support. He had changed. The man who had once been distant was now here, with me, for this moment—the birth of our child.

The hospital room was filled with a quiet urgency, the soft beeping of machines and the occasional murmur of nurses preparing for the delivery. The pain intensified with each passing hour, but the anticipation of holding our baby kept me going. Arjun stayed close, his hand in mine, even though I could see the fear in his eyes. He wasn't ready to be a father—not fully—but he was here, and that was enough for now.

"Ananya," he whispered, his voice strained, "you're doing great. We're almost there."

His words didn't offer much comfort, but his touch did. There was a tenderness in the way he held my hand, a gentleness that spoke volumes. I squeezed his fingers harder when another contraction hit, trying to ground myself in the moment.

The hours dragged on, but I wasn't giving up. The pain was excruciating, but it was a pain with purpose. It was the pain that brought our child into this world, the child who had already started to change everything about us.

Finally, after what felt like an eternity, the moment came. The room was filled with the sound of the baby's first cry, loud and strong. And in that instant, all the pain, all the fear, melted away. I couldn't stop the tears that streamed down my face as I looked at the tiny form in the nurse's arms, wrapped snugly in a blanket. My son. Our son.

"The cry of life, so pure, so loud,
Breaking through the silent shroud,
A promise, a hope, a new refrain,
In his first breath, we heal our pain."

I could see the way Arjun's eyes lit up when the nurse placed our baby in his arms. The man who had once been so detached, so unsure, now held our child with a tenderness I had never seen before. I watched him, taking in the wonder in his eyes, the way he marveled at our son's tiny hands and feet. At that moment, I knew something had shifted in him—something deeper than he had allowed himself to feel before.

"He's perfect," Arjun whispered, his voice thick with emotion.

I couldn't help but smile through my tears. It was the first time in months that I saw the Arjun I once knew—the man who could love with all his heart, the man who was capable of warmth and kindness. And as I looked at our son in his arms, I realized that, perhaps, we had both been waiting for this moment to truly start healing.

I reached out, gently caressing my baby's cheek, feeling the warmth of his soft skin.

"We did it, Arjun," I said softly, my voice barely above a whisper. "We have our son."

He nodded, his gaze never leaving the baby. "We did," he said, his voice thick with emotion. "And I promise, Ananya, I'll be here for both of you. I'll be here for him... and for you."

I smiled, exhaustion taking over my body, but my heart felt lighter than it had in a long time. The road ahead would still be challenging, but I no longer feared the unknown. I wasn't alone in this anymore. Arjun had found a way back to us, and together, we would navigate the uncertain waters of parenthood.

And as I held our baby, our beautiful baby boy, I couldn't help but think that this was just the beginning. It wasn't just a new chapter for our family; it was a chance for us to rebuild—one step at a time.

In that small hospital room, surrounded by the hum of machines and the soft cries of our child, I knew one thing for sure: we were going to make it. Together.

The day of my labor, the day of our son's birth, would always be etched in my heart. It wasn't just the day our child came into the world—it was the day our family was born. And with it, the hope of a new beginning.

Ananya had been feeling overwhelmed, but now, with their son in her arms, everything felt right. The pain of the past had faded, replaced by a quiet, warm joy she hadn't known was possible. She reached for her phone, needing to share the news with Kabir, who had been a constant source of support through her journey with Arjun.

"Hey Kabir," she said softly, her voice full of emotion, "I just wanted to let you know... Arjun and I did it. It's a boy. Our son is here. And Arjun... he's here too. Everything's changing, and I feel like, for the first time in a long while, things are right."

Kabir paused for a moment, then replied, "Ananya, that's the most beautiful news I've heard. I'm so happy for you both. You've come so far, and it's all leading to this... to new beginnings."

The next day, Kabir sat in front of the FM radio, a sense of peace settling over him as he prepared to share Ananya's story. He spoke into the microphone, his voice smooth and comforting, the weight of his words filling the air.

"In the quiet moments between pain and hope, a story unfolds. A tale of love, of change, and of second chances," Kabir began. *"Ananya's life was a journey filled with uncertainty, but in the end, it led her to a place of happiness and healing. And not just for her, but for Arjun too—who found a way back to her and their child. Together, they embraced the future, a future that now had the bright, shining face of their son. Life has a way of surprising us, of shifting and evolving. And sometimes, the greatest gifts come when we least expect them. So here's to new beginnings, to love that grows and to a family born not just of blood, but of hope."*

He paused, a soft smile on his face as he wrapped up his words with a poetic touch.

"From the storm, a rainbow rises,
In the darkest skies, the sun surprises.
Through pain and tears, love finds its way,
And in the end, we see the light of day.
Ananya's story is just the start,
Of a journey bound by a loving heart."

And with that, Kabir turned off the mic, his heart full of warmth, knowing that Ananya's life had changed forever—and that, somehow, he had been a part of it.

Epilouge

I wrote this novel to show how one painful secret can change a life. I named it A Knot Of Secrets because of a very important moment in Ananya's life—her wedding night. Instead of a happy beginning, that night turned tragic when her husband revealed that he married her only because of family pressure, not true love. That single revelation became the knot tying together all her struggles with family, love, and unclear path of life.

As I wrote Ananya's story, I learned that even the most painful secrets can help us grow stronger. Despite facing many challenges and little support from her partner, Ananya remained strong against all odds and waited patiently for her husband's love to bloom again. In today's world, when so many couples are drifting apart or choosing divorce, I believe every couple should consider the long-lasting emotional effects on themselves, their children, and their future. Divorce is not always the answer; open communication and standing together through every challenge are key to a lasting marriage.

For me, A Knot Of Secrets reminds us that our darkest truths, though hard to face, can eventually lead us to a better future. Even in the most difficult moments, there is a chance for healing, hope, and growth when we choose to stick together and work through our problems with patience and commitment.